Vegan Keto Meal Plan & Cookbook for Women Over 50 [3 Books in 1]

150+ Ready-to-Go Meals, Gourmet Dishes and High-Protein Recipes for Healthy Low-Carb Living

By

Jamie Carter

Author : Jamie Carter

Jamie Carter is a nutritionist who specializes in the ketogenic diet and exercise physiology in 2015. He struggled with his health and her weight in childhood which led to her becoming such a passionate nutrition expert. "My goal is to help transform people lives and start living again!" Jamie spends most of his time with clients around the world via online coaching with amazing and measurable results. She specializes in helping autoimmune diseases, diabetes (type 1 and type 2), heart disease, cholesterol problems, alopecia, cancer, epilepsy, seizures, depression and anxiety. You'd be amazed at the number of people who stop taking drugs with her guidance. She helped thousands of clients over the past 5 years.

She is also an author of over 30 books from the 2 massive series: "Air Fryer Boot Camp" & "The Rules of Ketogenic Life", currently available!

Table of Contents

THE HEALTHY KETO MEAL PREP COOKBOOK WITH PICTURES

VEGAN KETO MEAL PLAN COOKBOOK WITH PICTURES

THE COMPLETE KETOGENIC GUIDEBOOK FOR WOMEN OVER 50

The Healthy Keto Meal Prep Cookbook with Pictures

Bend the Rules to Lose Weight Tasting Tens of Easy-to-Prep Ketogenic Recipes On a Budget

By

Jamie Carter

Table of Contents

Introduction

Few aspects are as well known in nutrition research as the tremendous health advantages of low-carb and ketogenic diets. Not only can these diets increase the cholesterol, blood pressure and blood sugar, but they also reduce your appetite, promote weight control and decrease the triglycerides.

A ketogenic diet may be an interesting way to manage such disorders and could accelerate weight loss. Yet it is challenging to follow, because it may be high on red meat and other oily, dried, and salty foods that are notoriously unhealthy. We still may not know anything about the long-term consequences, presumably because it's too hard to stay with that people can't eat this way for a long time. It is also important to note that "yo-yo diets" that contribute to rapid weight loss fluctuation are correlated with increased mortality. Instead of joining in the next common diet that will last just a few weeks or months (for most people that requires a ketogenic diet), strive to accept progress that is manageable over the long term. A healthy, unprocessed diet, abundant in very colorful fruits and vegetables, lean meats, seafood, whole grains, almonds, peas, olive oil, and plenty of water seems to provide the strongest evidence for a long, healthier, vibrant existence.

If you're interested to improve your fitness, this diet book might be worth considering.

Chapter 1: Keto Diet

The ketogenic (keto) diet is commonly known for having a diet (low crab), where the body creates ketones in the liver to be used as energy. It's alluded to by several different names – ketogenic diet, low carb diet, low carb high fat (LCHF), etc. When you consume something rich in carbohydrates, the body can release glucose and insulin.

Glucose is the simplest molecule for the body to transform and use as energy such that it can be preferred over some other energy source.

Insulin is created to process the glucose in your bloodstream by taking it across the body.

The glucose is being used as primary energy; the fats are not required and are thus processed. Usually, on a regular, higher carbohydrate diet, the body can use glucose as the key energy source. By lowering the consumption of carbohydrates, the body is induced into a condition known as ketosis. Ketosis, a normal mechanism the body initiates to help us live while food consumption is limited. During this state, we create ketones, which are formed by the oxidation of fats in the liver.

The ultimate aim of a well-controlled keto diet is to push your body into this physiological condition. We don't do this by deprivation of calories or starvation of carbohydrates.

What Do I Eat on a Keto Diet?

To initiate a keto diet, you may want to prepare accordingly. That implies getting a viable diet plan ready a. What you consume depends on how quickly you choose to get into a ketogenic condition, i.e., ketosis. The further stringent you are on your carbohydrates (less than 25g net carbs a day), the sooner you can reach ketosis.

You want to keep your carbs limited, come more from fruits, nuts, and dairy. Don't consume some processed grains such as wheat (bread, pasta, and cereals), starch (potatoes, beans, legumes) or berries. The small exceptions to this are banana, star fruit, and berries which may be eaten in moderation.

Do Not Eat

Grains: grain, maize, cereal, rice, etc.

Sugar: honey, maple syrup, agave, etc.

Fruit: bananas, grapes, strawberries, etc.

Tubers: yams, potatoes, etc.

Do Eat

Meats: fish, meat, lamb, chickens, chickens, etc.

Leafy Greens: lettuce, cabbage, etc.

Vegetables: broccoli, cauliflower, etc.

Low Fat Dairy: strong cheeses, high-fat milk, butter, etc.

Nuts and seeds: macadamias, walnuts, sunflower seeds, etc.

Avocado and berries – raspberries, blackberries, and other low glycemic

Sweeteners: stevia, erythritol, monk berries, and other low-carb sweeteners

Other fats: palm oil, high-fat salad dressing, fatty fats, etc.

Benefits of a Ketogenic Diet

Several advantages come from being on keto: from weight reduction and improved energy levels to medicinal uses. Mostly, everyone can easily profit from consuming a low-carb, high-fat diet. Below, you'll find a concise list of the advantages you may get from a ketogenic diet.

Weight Loss

The ketogenic diet actually utilizes your body fat as an energy source – but there are clear weight-loss advantages. On keto, your insulin (the fat-storing hormone) level drops greatly and transforms your body into a fat-burning process. Scientifically, the ketogenic diet has demonstrated better outcomes relative to low-fat and high-carb diets, also in the long run.

Control Blood Sugar

Keto reduces blood sugar levels due to the kinds of diet you consume. Studies also suggest that the ketogenic diet is a more efficient way to treat and avoid diabetes relative to low-calorie diets.

If you're pre-diabetic or have Type II diabetes, you should strongly try a ketogenic diet. We have several readers who have had experience in their blood sugar management on keto.

Mental Focus

Many people use the ketogenic diet primarily for improved mental output. Ketones are a perfect source of food for the brain. When you reduce carb consumption, you stop major increases in blood sugar. Together, which will help in increased attention and concentration? Studies suggest that an improved consumption of fatty acids may have affecting benefits to our brain's function.

Increased Energy & Normalized Hunger

By providing your body a stronger and more stable energy supply, you can feel more energized throughout the day. Fats are the most powerful molecule to burn as heat. On top of that, fat is inherently more rewarding and ends up keeping us in a satiated ("full") condition for longer.

Types of Ketogenic Diets

Many people wonder whether carbs are required to grow muscle. Actually, they're not. If you're asking this question, I will presume you know how you accumulate mass.

Your glycogen reserves will also be refilled while on a ketogenic diet. A keto diet is an effective way to grow muscle, but protein consumption is essential here. It's proposed that if you are trying to grow muscle, you could be getting in between 1.0 – 1.2g protein per lean pound of body mass. Putting muscle on can be slower on a ketogenic diet, but that's because the overall body fat is not growing as much.

If, for any reason, you need to add on body fat, too, you will accomplish your targets by various forms of a Ketogenic Diet. There are:

Standard Ketogenic Diet (SKD): This is the classic keto diet that everybody understands and does.

Targeted Ketogenic Diet (TKD): This variant is where you consume SKD but ingest a limited amount of fast-digesting carbohydrates before a workout.

Cyclical Ketogenic Diet (CKD): This variant of keto for bodybuilders and contests goers, usually offering one day a week to carb up and resupplies glycogen stocks.

Common Side Effects of a Keto Diet

Here are some of the more popular side effects that one comes across when people first initiate keto. Frequently the problems contribute to dehydration or loss of micronutrients (vitamins) in the body. Be sure that you're consuming enough water (close to a gallon a day) and enjoying foods containing healthy sources of micronutrients.

Cramps

Cramps (and, more importantly, leg cramps) are a fairly normal occurrence before beginning a ketogenic diet. It's typically happening in the morning or at night, but overall, it's a fairly small concern. It's a warning that there's a shortage of minerals, especially magnesium, in the body. Be sure you consume lots of fluid and eat salt on your meal. Using so will help reduce the lack of magnesium and get rid of the problem.

Constipation

The most frequent source of constipation is dehydration. An easy approach is to maximize water consumption and aim to get as close to a gallon a day as possible.

Trying to make sure veggies have some fiber. Bringing in some high-quality fiber from non-starchy vegetables will fix this issue. Though if that's not enough, normally, psyllium husk powder can work or take a probiotic.

Heart Palpitations

When switching to keto, you may find that the heart is beating both faster and slower. It's fairly normal, so don't think about it. If the condition remains, make sure that you're consuming enough liquids and eating enough salt. Usually, this is adequate to get rid of the issue right away. Though if the problem continues, it might be worth having a potassium supplement once a day.

Reduced Physical Performance

You can have some restrictions on your results when you start a keto diet, but it's generally only from your body transitioning to using fat, when your body changes in utilizing fat for energy, all of your power and stamina will return to normal. If you still notice issues with results, you can see benefits from taking carbs before exercising (or cycling carbs).

Saving Money and Budgeting

A popular myth is that the ketogenic diet is more costly than most diets out there. And, though it can be a little bit more costly than eating grain-stuffed goods, it's still better than many people believe. A ketogenic diet can be more costly than a regular American diet, but it's no different than most clean eating lifestyles. That said, there are always several ways to save money when cooking keto. The key strategies to raise money are the same as in all other budgeting:

Look for offers. There's still a discount or an offer to be had on keto-friendly products out there. Usually, you can find substantial discounts in magazines and newspapers that are delivered to your home, but they can also be paired with in-store specials and manager cuts. As paired, you will save a large portion of your keto groceries.

Bulk purchase and cook. If you're somebody who doesn't want to invest a lot of time in the kitchen, this is the best in all worlds. Buying the food at volume (specifically from wholesalers) will reduce the cost per pound immensely. Plus, you can make ahead food (bulk cook chicken thighs for pre-made beef, or cook whole meals) that are used as leftovers, meaning you waste less time preparing.

Do stuff yourself. Although it's incredibly easy to purchase certain products pre-made or pre-cooked, it still contributes to the price per pound of goods. Try prepping vegetables ahead of time instead of getting pre-cut ones. Try having your stew meat from a chuck roast. Or attempt to produce your mayo and salad dressings at home. The easiest of items will operate to cut back on your overall food shopping.

How to Reach Ketosis

Achieving ketosis is fairly simple, but it may appear complex and overwhelming for all of the details out there. Here's the bottom line about what you need to do, arranged in stages of importance:

Restrict the sugars: Many people prefer to only rely only on net carbohydrates. If you want better outcomes, restrict both. Aim to remain below 20g net carbs and below 35g gross carbs a day.

Restrict the protein consumption: Some people come over to keto from an Atkins diet and don't restrict their protein. Too much protein can contribute to lower levels of ketosis. Ideally, you ought to eat between 0.6g and 0.8g protein per pound of lean body fat. To assist with this, try using the keto calculator >

Stop thinking about fat: Fat is the main source of calories on keto – just be sure you're giving the body plenty of it. You should not lose weight on keto by malnutrition.

Drink water: Aim to drink a gallon of water a day. Make sure that you're hydrating and remaining compliant with the volume of water you consume. It not only helps regulate many important bodily functions, but it also helps manage hunger levels.

Stop snacking: Weight reduction seems to perform well because you have fewer insulin surges during the day. Unnecessary snacking can lead to stalls or delays in development.

Start fasting: Fasting can be a perfect tool to raise ketone levels reliably during the day. There are several different ways to go about it. Add workout in. It's a proven reality that exercise is safer. If you want to get the best out of your ketogenic diet, try putting in 20-30 minutes of workout a day. Also, only a short stroll will help control weight loss and blood sugar levels.

Begin supplementing: Although not normally required, supplementing can aid with a ketogenic diet.

What the Science Tell Us about the Keto Diet

The keto diet has been used to better treat epilepsy, a condition marked by seizures, for more than 100 years. More current trials are investigating the keto diet as an effective nutritional therapy for obesity and diabetes. Clinical results on the effects of the keto diet on these health problems are exceedingly minimal. Studies on the success of the keto diet are performed with limited groups of participants. And, much of the research on Alzheimer's disease depends on testing conducted on experimental animals. To completely evaluate the protection of this eating style, further study is required. Plus, research must be performed on the long-term health implications of the keto diet. Body mass index and human metabolic rates affect how easily various people generate ketones. This suggests that certain individuals lose weight more slowly with the keto diet than others even though they are pursuing the same keto diet schedule. For this community of individuals, the keto diet may be stressful and can affect their enthusiasm for making healthy lifestyle improvements. Plus, many individuals are not willing to continue with the keto diet and gain back weight after adjusting to their former eating style.

Chapter 2: Keto Diet Breakfast Recipes

Keto Hot Chocolate

YIELDS: 1

TOTAL TIME: 0 HOURS **20** MINS.

INGREDIENTS

- • 2 Tbsp. of cocoa powder, and more for flavor
- • 2 1/2 Tsp. of sugar keto (diet), (such as swerve)
- • 1 1/4 c. of Water
- • 1/4 c. of heavy cream
- • 1/4 Tsp. of Pure vanilla bean paste
- • Whipped serum, for serving

DIRECTIONS

1. In a small saucepan over medium-low heat, whisk together swerve, cocoa powder or about 2 Tbs. water until smooth and dissolved. Increase heat to medium, add remaining water and cream, and whisk until cook.

2. Mix the chocolate then pour into cup. Serve with whipped cream and a dusting of sugar powder.

Keto Sausage Breakfast Sandwich

YIELDS: 3

TOTAL TIME: 0 HOURS 15 MINS

INGREDIENTS

- 6 large size eggs
- 2 Tbsp. of heavy cream
- Pinch of red chili flakes
- Salt (kosher)
- Finely roasted black pepper
- 1 Tbsp. of butter
- 3 slices of cheddar
- 6 packaged of sausage burgers, cooked as per box directions
- Avocado, sliced

DIRECTIONS

1. Take a small bowl beat eggs, red chili flakes and heavy cream jointly. Season with pepper and salt. Melt the butter in fry pan at low flame. Add around one third of eggs in to pan. Add a piece of cheese in the center or let stay for 1 minute. Roll the ends of egg in to center, filling a cheese. Take out from heat and continue with leftover egg.

2. Serve eggs in 2 sausage buns with avocado.

Keto Breakfast Cups

YIELDS: 12

TOTAL TIME: 0 HOURS **40** MINS

INGREDIENTS

- 2 Ib. of Pork (ground)
- 1 Tbsp. thyme, finely sliced
- 2 cloves of garlic, finely chopped
- 1/2 Tsp. of Paprika
- 1/2 Tsp. of cumin, ground
- 1 Tsp. of Salt kosher
- Black pepper softly roasted
- 21/2 cup of clean minced spinach
- 1 c. of cheddar, thinly sliced
- Eggs, 12
- 1 Tbsp. of chives that are finely cut

DIRECTIONS

1. 1 Preheat the oven at 400 degrees. Combine the thyme, ground pork, paprika, garlic, salt, and cumin in a large size cup.
2. In each muffin container, add a tiny handful of pork and push up the sides to make a cup. Split the cheese and spinach equally in cups. Break the egg and add the salt and pepper on the top of each cup. Cook for around 25 minutes until the eggs are fixed and the sausage is fried.
3. Garnish and serve with chives.

Best-Ever Cabbage Hash Browns

YIELDS: 2

TOTAL TIME: 0 HOURS **25** MINS

INGREDIENTS

- 2 Large size eggs
- 1/2 Tsp. of garlic, powdered
- 1/2 Tsp. of salt (kosher)
- Freshly roasted black pepper
- 2c. of cabbage that is shredded
- ¼ of small size yellow onions, finely chopped
- 1 Tbsp. of oil (vegetable)

DIRECTIONS

1. Whisk the garlic powder, salt, and eggs together in a large cup. Add black pepper for seasoning. In egg mixture add onion and cabbage and toss to mix properly.
2. Heat oil in a large frying pan. Split the mixture in the pan into 4 patties and press spatula to soften. Cook until soft and golden, around three minutes on each side.

Chocolate Keto Protein Shake

YIELD: 1

TOTAL TIME: 0 HOURS **5** MINS

INGREDIENTS

- 3/4 c of almond milk
- 1/2 c. of ice
- 2 Tbsp. of Butter (almond)
- 2 Tbsp. of (Sugar free) powder of cocoa
- 3 Tbsp. of keto-diet sugar substitute as per taste (such as Swerve)
- 1Tbsp. seeds of chia or more for serving
- 2 Tbsp. seeds of hemp, or more for serving
- 1/2 Tbsp. of pure vanilla (extracted)
- Salt kosher as per taste

DIRECTIONS

1. Merge all of blending mixture and mix untill soft. Put into glass and serve with hemp seed and chia.

Hard Boiled Egg

YIELDS: 1

TOTAL TIME: 0 HOURS **20** MINS

INGREDIENTS

- 12 large size eggs
- Some water

DIRECTIONS

1. Place the eggs in such a wide saucepan and cover them with one inch of ice water. Keep the saucepan on the burner and get it to a boil. Immediately turn off the flame and cover the saucepan. Let settle down for eleven minutes.
2. Take it out from the pan and switch it to ice water. Until serving or peeling, let it cool for 2 minutes.

Paleo Breakfast Stacks

YIELDS: 3

TOTAL TIME: 0 HOURS 30 MINS

INGREDIENTS

- 3 sausage buns for breakfast
- 1 avocado, finely mashed
- Salt (kosher)
- Black pepper freshly roasted
- 3 large size eggs
- Chives, (for serving)
- Hot sauce, if ordered

DIRECTIONS

1. Cook the breakfast sausage as per the box's instructions.
2. Mash the avocado over the sausage for breakfast and season with pepper and salt.
3. Use cooking oil to spray the medium size pan then spray the interior of mason jar cover. Place the mason jar lid in the middle of the pan and crack the interior of an egg. Add pepper or salt and cook until the whites are set for 3 minutes, then remove the cover and begin to cook.
4. Place the egg on top of the avocado puree. Serve with chives and drizzle with your favorite spicy hot sauce.

Ham & Cheese Breakfast Roll-Ups

YIELDS: 2

TOTAL TIME: 0 HOURS **20** MINS

INGREDIENT

- 4 large size eggs
- 1/4 c of milk
- 2 Tbsp. of finely cut chives
- Salt (kosher)
- Black pepper freshly roasted
- 1Tbsp. of butter
- 1c. of cheddar shredded,(Split)
- 4 slices of ham

DIRECTIONS

1. Whisk the milk, chives, and egg together in a medium cup. Add pepper or salt.
2. Melt the butter in a medium pan over low heat. Put 1/2 of the egg mixture in the pan and shift to make a thin layer that covers the whole plan.
3. Cook for two minutes. Add1/2 cup of cheddar or seal again for 2 minutes, before the cheese has melted transfer to plate, and put 2 slices of ham or rolls them. Repeat and cook with the rest of the ingredients.

Cauliflower Toast

YIELDS: 4 - 6

TOTAL TIME: 0 HOURS **45** MINS

INGREDIENTS

- 1 cauliflower (in medium size)
- Large size egg
- 1/2 c. of cheddar cheese (shredded)
- 1Tsp.of garlic(powdered)
- Salt (kosher)
- Black pepper freshly roasted

DIRECTIONS

1. Set the oven at 425 degree temperature and cover the baking sheet with parchment paper. Finely chopped the cauliflower and switch to a large size cup. Set the microwave at high temperature for 8 minutes. Drain with cheesecloth and paper towels just before the mixture is dry.
2. In cauliflower cup, add the cheddar, garlic powder and egg and season with pepper and salt. Mix it until joint
3. Make a cauliflower into bread forms on prepared baking sheet and bake for 18 to 20 minutes until golden.
4. Switch to a plate cover with the appropriate topping, such as fried egg, mashed avocado, tomato, broccoli, and sausage.

Breakfast Bacon and Egg Salad

YIELDS: 4

TOTAL TIME: 0 HOURS **30** MINS

INGREDIENTS

Bacon vinaigrette

- 4 bacon (slices)
- 1 shallot, thinly sliced
- 3 Tbsp. of red wine(vinegar)
- 1 Tsp. of mustard (Dijon)
- 1/4 Tsp. of salt (kosher)
- 1/4 Tsp. of black pepper
- 4 Tbsp. of Oil

Salad

2 small size eggs
1 Spinach (package)
1/4 c. of crumbled feta
1 pt. of tomatoes and cherry

DIRECTIONS

1. In a large fry pan, cook the bacon. Remove the bacon slices and put on a plate and line with towel paper to drain. Implode half of the bacon until the excess fat has drained, then cut the rest of two pieces into large pieces. Set again.

2. Making the vinaigrette: Add the shallot into the pot in which the bacon has been fried, and sauté for around 1 minute over moderate flame until golden brown. Pour the shallots into a small cup and blend with the pepper, salt, red vinegar, and mustard. Whisk in the oil, and then add the crumbled bacon and blending to combine. Set again.

3. In the same pot, fried each egg and cook until the egg white is fixed.

4. Assemble the salad: Combine the feta, lettuce, tomatoes, cherry, spinach and the remaining sliced bacon in a large size dish. Cover with vinaigrette.
5. Place the salad in two cups and cover it with the fried egg. Immediately serve.

Keto Blueberry Muffins

YIELD: 1

TOTAL TIME: 0 HOURS **40** MINS

INGREDIENTS

- 2 1/2 c. of almond Flour
- 1/3 c. of Keto diet sugar (such as Swerve)
- 1 1/2 Tsp. of baking powder
- 1/2 Tsp. of baking soda
- 1/2 Tsp. salt kosher
- 1/3 c. of melted butter
- 1/3 c. of Sugar free almonds milk
- 3 large size eggs
- 1 Tsp. of pure vanilla extract
- 2/3 of c. of fresh blueberries
- ½ of lemon zest (as an option)

DIRECTIONS

1. Preheat oven to 350° and line a 12-cup muffin pan with cupcake liners.
2. In a large bowl, whisk to combine baking powder, baking soda, almond flour, salt kosher and swerve. Whisk in eggs, vanilla, almond milk, melted butter and almond milk until just together.

3. Gently fold   lemon zest (if using) and blueberries until uniformly divided. Scoop uniform quantity of butter into every cupcake liner and cook until slightly   golden brown and insert a toothpick into the middle of a muffin comes out clean, 23 minutes. Let cool slightly before presenting.

Mason Jar Omelets

YIELDS: 2

TOTAL TIME: 0 HOURS **15** MINS

INGREDIENTS

- Nonstick cooking oil
- 4 large size eggs
- 2/3 c. of cheddar shredded
- ½ of onion, thinly sliced
- 1 Chopped capsicum
- 1/2 c. of ham (sliced)
- Salt kosher
- Freshly roasted black pepper
- 1Tbsp. of Chives that are finely sliced

DIRECTIONS

1. Oil the nonstick baking spray into two liter mason jars.
2. Break two eggs into each jar. Between two jar divide the onion, ham capsicum, and cheese and season with pepper and salt.
3. Put cover on jar and mix until eggs are scrambled and all ingredients are mixed.
4. Remove the cover and   place in the oven. Microwave for 4 minutes on low flame, and looking every 30 seconds. Garnish with chives, and serve immediately.

Keto Fat Bombs

YIELDS: 16

TOTAL TIME: 0 HOURS **30** MIN

INGREDIENTS

- 8 oz. of cream cheese, mitigated at room temp.
- 1/2 c. of keto diet (peanuts) butter
- 1/4 c of (coconut oil)
- 1/4 Tsp. of salt (kosher)
- 1/2 c. of dark chocolate (keto diet) (such as Lily's)

DIRECTIONS

1. Cover the baking sheet with a tiny parchment paper. Mix the peanut butter, salt, cream cheese and 1/4 cup of coconut oil in a medium dish. With the help of hand blender beat the mixture for around 2 minutes until all   ingredients are properly mixed. Keep the dish for 10 to 15 minutes in the freezer to firm up slightly.
2. Using a tiny cookie spoon or scoop to make a Tbs. sized balls until the (peanut butter) mixture has been settled. Keep in the freezer for 5 minutes to harden.
3. Besides that, making a drizzle of chocolate: mix the cocoa powder and the leftover coconut oil in a safe microwave dish and cook for 30 seconds until completely melt. Drizzle over the balls of peanut butter and put them back in the fridge to harden for 5 minutes.
4. Keep the cover and freeze it for storage purpose.

Cloud Eggs

YIELDS: 4

TOTAL TIME: 0 HOURS 20 MINS

INGREDIENTS

- 8 large size eggs
- 1 c. of Parmesan, thinly sliced
- 1/2 lb. of Ham deli, diced
- Salt (kosher)
- Freshly made black pepper
- For serving, finely sliced chives

DIRECTIONS

1. Heat the oven at 450 °C and spread cooking oil on a large baking sheet. Separate the yolks and egg whites, yolks are keep in small cup and egg whites are keep in large cup egg whites. Use a hand blender or whisk break egg whites before stiff peaks shape and cook for 3 minutes. Fold in the ham and parmesan or season with pepper and salt.
2. Spoon the 8 mounds of egg onto the heated baking dish and indent centers to make nests. Cook for around 3 minutes, until lightly golden.
3. Spoon the egg yolk cautiously into the middle of each nest, then season with pepper or salt. Cook for around 3 minutes more until the yolks are ready.
4. Before presenting, garnish it with chives.

Chapter 3: Keto Diet Lunch Recipes

Cobb Egg Salad

YIELDS: 6

TOTAL TIME: 0 HOURS **20** MINS

INGREDIENTS

- 3 Tbsp. of mayonnaise
- 3 Tbsp. of yogurt
- 2 tbsp. of vinegar with red wine
- Salt (kosher)
- Black pepper freshly roasted
- 8 hard-boiled eggs, sliced into 8 pieces, and more for garnishing.
- 8 bacon strips, fried and crumbled, and more for garnishing.
- 1 avocado, cut finely
- 1/2 c. of blue cheese, crumbled, and more for garnishing
- 1/2 c. of halved cherry tomatoes, and more for garnishing
- 2 Tbsp. of chives that are finely chopped

DIRECTIONS

1. Mix the yogurt, red vinegar and mayonnaise together in a small cup. Seasoning with pepper and salt.
2. Mix the avocado, bacon, eggs, pineapple, cherry tomatoes and blue cheese, softly together in a large serving cup. Gently roll in the mayonnaise coating until the all ingredients are finely coated, and then sprinkle with pepper and salt.
3. Serving with chives and supplementary toppings

Taco Stuffed Avocado

YIELDS: 4 - 8

TOTAL TIME: 0 HOURS 25 MINS

INGREDIENTS

- 4 large size avocados
- 1 lime juice
- 1 Tbsp. of olive oil (extra-virgin)
- 1 medium size onion, minced
- 1 lb. minced meat of beef
- 1 taco seasoning pack
- Salt (kosher)
- Blinerack pepper freshly roasted
- 2/3 of c. of chopped Mexican cheese
- 1/2 c. of chopped Lettuce
- 1/2 c. of Grape tomatoes (Sliced)
- Sour milk, for garnishing

DIRECTIONS

1. Pit and halve the avocados halve and pit. Scoop out a bit of avocado with the help of a spoon, forming a wide layer. Dice extracted avocado and later put aside for use. Pinch the lime juice (to avoid frying!) at all the avocados.

2. Heat the oil in a medium size pan over medium heat. Add the onion and roast for around 5 minutes, until soft. Break up the meat with a wooden spatula then add ground beef and taco for seasoning. Sprinkle with pepper and salt, and roast for around 6 minutes until the beef is no more pink. Drain the fat after removing from the heat.

3. Fill up the each avocado halve with meat, then and coat with cheese, reserved avocado, tomato, onion, lettuce, and a dollop of sour cream.

Buffalo Shrimp Lettuce Wraps

YIELDS: 4

TOTAL TIME: 0 HOURS **35** MINS

INGREDIENTS

- 1/4 Tbsp. of butter
- 2 cloves of garlic, chopped
- 1/4 c. of Hot sauce, for example, Frank's
- 1 Tbsp. of olive oil (extra-virgin)
- 1 lbs. of Chopped and finely diced shrimp, tails (cut)
- Salt kosher
- Black pepper freshly roasted
- 1 head Romaine, different leaves, for garnishing
- 1/4 of red onion, finely minced
- 1 rib celery, finely chopped
- 1/2 c. of Crumbled blue cheese

DIRECTIONS

1. Making the buffalo sauce: Melt the butter in a small pan. When fully melted, then add chopped garlic and simmer for 1 minute, until golden brown. Add hot sauce and stir together. Switch the heat to low whilst the shrimp is frying.
2. Making shrimp: Heat oil in a large frying pan. Put some shrimp and sprinkle with pepper and salt. Cook, turning midway, until both sides are opaque and pink, around 2 minutes on each side. Turn off the flame and add the (buffalo) sauce and toss to fill.
3. Prepare wraps: In the middle of the romaine leaf add a little scoop of shrimp, then coat with celery, blue cheese and red onion.

Keto Broccoli Salad

YIELDS: 4
TOTAL TIME: 0 HOURS **35** MINS
INGREDIENTS

For the salad:

- Salt (kosher)
- 3 broccoli heads, sliced into bite-size parts
- 1/2 c. of cheddar shredded
- 1/4 red onion, finely cut
- 1/4 c. of   almonds sliced (baked)
- 3 bacon slices, fried and crumbled
- 2 Tbsp. of Chives that are finely cut

For the dressing:

- 2/3 of c. of mayonnaise
- 3 Tbsp. of   Vinegar (Apple Cider)
- 1 Tbsp. of Mustard dijon
- salt kosher
- Black pepper freshly roasted

DIRECTIONS

1. Bring the 6 cups of (salted) water to a boil in a medium pot or frying pan. Prepare a big bowl of ice water while waiting for the water to heat.
2. Put some broccoli florets to the boiling water and simmer for 1 to 2 minutes, until soft. Detach with a slotted spoon,   and put in the prepared ice water cup. Drain the florets in a colander while it is cold.
3. In a medium dish, whisk together the ingredients for the dressing. Season with pepper and salt to taste.
4. In a large bowl, combine all the salad ingredients and pour over the coating. Toss before the components are coated in the dressing. Refrigerate until prepared

Keto Bacon Sushi

YIELDS: 12

TOTAL TIME: 0 HOURS **30** MINS

INGREDIENTS

- 6 bacon pieces, (halved)
- 2 Persian cucumbers, cut finely
- 2 medium size carrots, cut finely
- 1 avocado, in slices
- 4 oz. of melted cream cheese, (cooked)

DIRECTIONS

1. Preheat oven to 400 ° degrees. Cover a baking sheet and match it with a cooling rack and aluminum foil. Put some bacon pieces in an even layer and cook for 11 to 13 minutes until mildly crisp but still pliable.
2. Mean a while, cut avocado, cucumbers, and broccoli into pieces around the width of bacon.
3. Spread an equal layer of cream cheese on each slice until the bacon is cold enough to touch it. Split up the vegetables between the bacon uniformly and put them on one side. Tightly roll up the vegetables.
4. Serve and garnish with sesame seeds.

Keto Burger Fat Bombs

YIELDS: 20

TOTAL TIME: 0 HOURS **30** MINS

INGREDIENTS

- Cooking oil
- 1 lbs. of ground-based meat
- 1/2 Tsp. of Powdered garlic
- Salt Kosher
- Black pepper freshly roasted
- 2 Tbsp. of cold butter,20 (sliced)
- 2 oz. of cheddar cheese 20 (sliced)
- Lettuce berries, meant for garnishing
- For garnishing, finely sliced tomatoes
- Mustard, for garnishing

DIRECTIONS

1. Preheat the oven at 375 °C and oil mini muffin container with cooking oil. And season the beef with garlic powder, salt, and pepper in a medium dish.
2. In the bottom of each muffin tin cup add the 1 Tsp. of beef equally, and fully covering the bottom. Place a layer of butter on top and add 1 Tsp. of beef over the butter to fully cover.
3. In each cup, place a slice of cheddar on top of the meat and place the remaining beef over the cheese to fully cover.
4. Bake for about 15 minutes, before the meat is ready. Let wait until cool.
5. Using a metal offset spoon carefully to release each burger out of the tin. Serve with salad leaves, mustard and onions.

Keto Taco Cups

YIELDS: 1 DOZEN

TOTAL TIME: 0 HOURS **30** MINS

INGREDIENTS

- 2 c. of Cheddar (Sliced) cheese
- 1 Tbsp. of Olive Oil (extra-Virgin)
- 1 small size chopped onion
- 3 cloves of garlic , finely chopped
- 1 lbs. of meat, ground
- 1 Tsp. of chili(in powdered form)
- 1/2 Tsp. of Cumin ,ground
- 1/2 tsp. of Paprika
- Salt (kosher)
- Black pepper freshly roasted
- Sour cream, to serve
- Diced avocado, planned for serving
- Cilantro finely chopped, for serving
- Tomatoes, chopped, for garnishing

DIRECTIONS

1. Preheat the oven to 375 ° and use parchment paper to cover a wide baking sheet. Add 2 teaspoons of cheddar a half inch away. Cook for around 6 minutes, until creamy and the edges begin to turn golden. Leave the baking sheet for a minute until cool.
2. Besides that, apply the oil in the muffin tin bottom with a cooking spray, then carefully pick up the slices of melted cheese and put them on the muffin tin bottom. Add another inverted muffin container until cool for 10 minutes. Using your hands to help shape the cheese around the twisted pan because you do not have a second muffin tin.
3. Preheat the large size pan over medium heat. Put the onion and simmer for around 5 minutes, mixing frequently, until soft. Whisk in the garlic, then add the ground beef to break up the beef with the help of wooden spoon. Cook for around 6 minutes, until the beef is no longer pink, and then drain the fat.
4. Place the meat back in the pan and season with cumin, chili powder, cinnamon, paprika, and pepper.
5. Move the cups of cheese into a serving bowl. Cover it with cooked ground beef and serve with cilantro, sour cream, tomatoes, and avocado.

Copycat Chicken Lettuce Wraps

YIELDS: 4

TOTAL TIME: 0 HOURS **30** MINS

INGREDIENTS

- 3 Tbsp. of Sauce (Hoisin)
- 2 Tbsp. Soy sauce (low-sodium)
- 2 Tbsp. vinegar from rice wine
- 1 Tbsp. of sriracha (as an option)
- 1 Tsp. oil with sesame seeds
- 1 Tbsp. olive oil (extra-virgin)
- 1 medium size chopped onion
- 2 cloves of garlic, chopped
- 1 Tbsp. of freshly coated ginger
- 1 lbs. of Chicken, ground
- 1/2 c. of drained and diced canned water chestnuts
- 2 green onions, cut finely
- Salt kosher
- Black pepper freshly roasted
- Large leafy lettuce for serving (leaves separated),
- Fried white rice, for garnishing(as an option)

DIRECTIONS

1. Making a sauce: Whisk together the soya sauce, the hoisin sauce, the sriracha the rice wine vinegar, the Sriracha and the sesame oil in a tiny cup.
2. Heat the olive oil in a large pan over a medium-high heat. Put some onions and cook for 5 minutes until soft, then stir the garlic and ginger and cook for 1 more minute until golden brown. Add ground chicken and cook until the meat is opaque and mostly finished, trying to break up the meat with a wooden spoon.

3. Add the sauce and simmer again for 1 or 2 minutes, before the sauce is slightly reduced and the chicken is thoroughly cooked. Switch off the flame, add green onions and chestnuts and mix. Season with pepper and salt.

4. Spoon rice and add a big scoop of chicken mixture (about 1/4 cup) into the middle of each lettuce leaf   (if used). Instantly serve

Egg Roll Bowls

YIELDS: 4

TOTAL TIME: 0 HOURS **35** MINS

INGREDIENTS

- 1 Tbsp. of oil for vegetables
- 1 clove of garlic, chopped
- 1 Tbsp. fresh ginger chopped
- 1 lbs. of pork, ground
- 1 Tbsp. of oil with sesame seeds
- 1/2 onion, cut finely
- 1 c. of Carrot(sliced)
- 1/4 green, thinly sliced (cabbage)
- 1/4 c. of soya sauce
- 1 Tbsp. of sriracha
- 1 small size green onion, finely chopped
- 1 Tbsp. of sesame seeds

DIRECTIONS

1. Heat the vegetable oil in a large skillet over medium heat. Add the garlic and ginger and roast for 1 to 2 minutes until it is moist. Add pork and roast until there is no more pink color has been shown.

2. Place the pork and add the sesame oil to other side. Add the tomato, cabbage, and potato. Add the soy sauce and Sriracha and whisk to combine with the beef. Cook for 5 to 8 minutes, until the cabbage is soft.

3. Garnish with sesame seeds and green onions and shift the mixture to a serving bowl. Serve immediately.

Caprese Zoodles

YIELDS: 4

TOTAL TIME: 0 HOURS **25** MINS

INGREDIENTS

- 4 large size zucchinis
- 2 Tbsp. of olive oil (extra-virgin)
- Kosher salt
- Black pepper freshly roasted
- 2 c. of cherry tomatoes, sliced in half
- 1 c. of mozzarella cubes, cut into pieces(if large)
- 1/4 c. fresh leaves of basil
- 2 Tbsp. of vinegar (balsamic)
- DIRECTIONS
1. Using a spiralizer, make zoodles with the help of zucchini.
2. In a large cup, add the zoodles mix with the olive oil, and add pepper and salt. Let them marinate for 15 minutes.
3. Add the basil, peppers, and mozzarella in zoodles and toss until mixed.
4. Drizzle and serve with balsamic.

Best-Ever Keto Quesadillas

YIELDS: 4

TOTAL TIME: 0 HOURS **35** MINS

INGREDIENTS

- 1 Tbsp. of olive oil (extra-virgin)
- 1 chopped bell pepper
- 1/2of onion(yellow), chopped
- 1/2 Tsp. of chili powdered
- Salt kosher
- Black pepper freshly roasted
- 3 c. of Monterey jack shredded
- 3 c. of cheddar cheese, shredded
- 4 c. of Chicken shredded
- 1 avocado, cut thinly
- 1 green onion, finely chopped
- Sour cream, for serving

DIRECTIONS

1. Preheat the oven to 400C and cover the parchment paper with two medium size baking sheets.
2. Heat the oil in a medium saucepan over medium heat. Season with salt, chili powder and pepper and add onion and pepper. Cook for 5 minutes, until it is tender. Transfer to a dish.
3. In a medium cup, mix the cheeses together. In the middle of both prepared baking sheets, add 1 1/2 cups of cheese mixture. Spread into an even coat and form the size of a flour tortilla into a circle.
4. Bake the cheeses for 8 to 10 minutes before they are melted and slightly golden along the sides. Add one half of   avocado slices, onion-pepper mixture, shredded chicken and avocado slices. Let it cool slowly, then use the small spoon and parchment paper and carefully fold and lift one end of the cheese

"tortilla" over the end with the topping. Return to the oven to heat for an extra 3 to 4 minutes. To make 2 more quesadillas, repeat the procedure.

5. Split each quesadilla into quarters. Before serving, garnish it with sour cream and green onion.

Cheeseburger Tomatoes

YIELDS: 4

TOTAL TIME: 0 HOURS **20** MINS

INGREDIENTS

- 1 Tbsp. of olive oil (extra-virgin)
- 1 medium size onion, minced
- 2 cloves of garlic, chopped
- 1 lbs. of ground-based meat
- 1 Tbsp. of ketchup
- 1 Tbsp. of mustard (Yellow)
- 4 sliced tomatoes
- Salt kosher
- Black paper freshly roasted
- 2/3 of c. of cheddar shredded
- 1/4 c. of Iceberg lettuce shredded
- 4 coins with pickles
- Seeds of sesame, for garnishing

DIRECTIONS

1. Heat oil in a medium pan over medium heat. Add the onion and cook for approximately 5 minutes until soft, then add the garlic. Add the ground beef, split up the meat with a wooden spoon and roast for around 6 minutes until the beef is no longer pink. Drain fats. Season with pepper and salt, then add the ketchup and mustard.

2. Because they are stem-side out, tossing tomatoes. Cut the tomatoes into six slices and be cautious not to cut the tomatoes full. Fold the slices carefully. Divide the tomatoes equally with the cooked ground beef, then fill it with lettuce and cheese.
3. Add sesame seeds and pickle coins for flavoring.

No-Bread Italian Subs

YIELDS: 6

TOTAL TIME: 0 HOURS **15** MINS

INGREDIENTS

- 1/2 c. of mayonnaise
- 2 Tbsp. of Vinegar with red wine
- 1 Tbsp. olive oil (extra-virgin)
- 1 tiny clove of garlic, finely chopped
- 1 Tsp. of seasoning (Italian)
- 6 slices of ham
- 12 salami sliced
- 12 pepperoni, sliced
- 6 provolone slices
- 1 c. of romaine(chopped)
- 1/2 c. of red peppers (roasted)

DIRECTIONS

1. Making a smooth Italian dressing: whisk the mustard, mayonnaise, garlic, oil, and Italian seasoning together in a small bowl until they are mixed.
2. Prepare the sandwiches: Layer a pieces of pork, two pieces of pepperoni, two pieces of salami and a piece of provolone.
3. In the center, add a handful of Romaine and a few roasted red peppers. Drizzle, with fluffy Italian sauce, then roll up and eat. Continue the procedure with the rest of the ingredients until you have 6 roll-ups.

California Burger Bowls

YIELDS: 4

TOTAL TIME: 0 HOURS **20** MINS

INGREDIENTS

For the dressing:

- 1/2 c. of olive oil (extra-virgin)
- 1/3 c. of vinegar (balsamic)
- 3Tbsp. of mustard dijon
- 2 Tsp. of. honey
- 1 clove of garlic , chopped
- Salt kosher
- Black pepper freshly roasted

For the burger:

- 1 lbs. of grass fed organic ground beef
- 1 Tsp. of Sauce (worcestershire)
- 1/2 tsp. of chili Powdered
- 1/2 tsp. onion Powdered
- Salt kosher
- Black pepper freshly roasted
- 1 packet of butter head lettuce
- 1 medium size red onion, sliced (¼)
- 1 avocado,(in pieces)
- 2 Walmart medium size tomato, thinly sliced

DIRECTIONS

1. Making the dressing: Whisk together the dressing components in a medium dish.
2. Making burgers: Mix beef with chili powder, (Worcestershire) sauce and onion powder in another large bowl. Season with salt and pepper and whisk until blend. Shape into 4 patties.

3. Heat a wide grill pan over medium heat and grill the onions until they are crispy and soft, around 3 minutes on at each end. Remove the grill from the pan and add the burgers. Bake until browned and fried to your taste on all ends, around 4 minutes per end for medium.

4. Assemble: Toss the lettuce with 1/2 of the dressing in a wide bowl and split between 4 bowls. Cover each with a patty of steak, tomatoes, fried onions, slices of 1/4 avocado. Drizzle and serve with the remaining dressing.

Chapter 4: Dinner Recipes

Keto Corned Beef & Cabbage

TOTAL TIME: 5 HOURS 0 MINS

YIELDS: 6

INGREDIENTS:

- 3 to 4 1bs. of corned beef
- Onions, 2 (quartered)
- 4 stalks of, quartered crosswise celery
- 1 pack of pickling spices
- Salt (Kosher)
- Black Pepper
- 1 medium size cabbage (green), sliced into 2 wedges
- carrots (2), sliced and split into 2" part
- 1/2 c. of Dijon mustard
- 2 Tbsp. of (apple cider) vinegar
- 1/4 c. of mayonnaise
- 2 Tbsp. capers, finely sliced, plus 1 tsp. of brine
- 2 Tbsp. of parsley, finely cut

Directions:

1. Place corned beef, onion, celery, and pickling spices into a large pot. Add the water to cover by 2", salt with season or Pepper, and bring to the boil. Medium heat, cover, and Simmer very (tender), 3–3 1/2 hours.
2. In the meantime, whisk Dijon mustard and apple cider vinegar in a small bowl and add salt and pepper. And in another bowl, mix capers, mayo, caper brine, and parsley. Season with salt and pepper

3. Added carrots and cabbage continue cooking for 45 minutes to 1 hour more until cabbage is soft. Remove meat, cabbage, and carrots from the pot. Piece of corned beef and season with a little more pepper and salt.
4. Present with both sauces on the side for soaking.

Keto Fried Chicken:

TOTAL TIME: 1 HOUR 15 MINS

YIELDS: 6 - 8

INGREDIENTS

FOR THE CHICKEN

- 6 (Bone-in), chicken breasts with skin, about 4 lbs.
- Salt (Kosher)
- Black Pepper, ground and fresh
- 2 large size eggs
- 1/2 c. of heavy cream
- 3/4 c. of almond flour
- 1 1/2 c. perfectly crushed pork rinds
- 1/2 c. of grated Parmesan, fresh
- 1 Tsp. of Garlic in powder form
- 1/2 Tsp. of paprika

FOR THE SPICY MAYO:

- 1/2 c. of Mayonnaise
- 1 1/2 Tsp. of Hot sauce

DIRECTIONS

1. Preheat oven to 400° and cover a wide baking sheet with parchment paper. Pat dry chicken with paper towels and add salt and pepper.

2. In a small bowl, mix together eggs and heavy cream. In another small dish, mix almond flour, pork rinds, Parmesan, garlic powder, and paprika. Add salt and black pepper.
3. Work at one time, soak the chicken in egg mix, then in the almonds flour mix, pressing to cover. Put the chicken on the lined baking dish.
4. Bake till chicken is gold and internal temp exceeds 165°, about 45 minutes.
5. In the meantime, produce dipping sauce: In a medium dish, mix mayonnaise and hot sauce. Add more hot sauce based on desired spiciness amount.
6. Serve chicken warm with dipping sauce.

Garlic Rosemary Pork Chops:

TOTAL TIME: 0 HOURS 30 MINS
YIELDS: 4
INGREDIENTS:
- 4 pieces of pork loin
- Salt (kosher)
- Black pepper freshly roasted
- 1Tbsp. of Freshly chopped rosemary
- 2 Garlic cloves, minced
- 1/2 c (1 stick) of butter melted
- 1 Tbsp. of Extra-virgin (olive oil)

DIRECTIONS:

1. Preheat the oven to 375 degrees. With salt and black pepper, season the pork chops generously.
2. Mix the honey, rosemary, and garlic together in a shallow dish. Only put back.
3. Heat the olive oil in an oven-safe skillet over (medium-high) heat and add the pork chops. Sear until golden for 4 minutes, flip and bake for a further 4 minutes. Pork chops are appropriately coated with garlic butter for 10-12 minutes.
4. Add more garlic butter to serve.

Keto Bacon Sushi

TOTAL TIME: 0 HOURS 30 MINS

YIELDS: 12

INGREDIENTS:

- 6 bacon strips, cut in half
- 2 cucumbers (Persian), cut thin
- 2 carrots (medium), cut thinly
- 1 (avocado), in slices
- 4 oz. (Creamy) cheese, cooked, soft
- Seeds of sesame (garnish)

DIRECTIONS:

1. Preheat the oven to 400 degrees. Line a baking sheet and match with a (cooling rack) with (aluminum) foil. Lay bacon half with an even surface and cook for 11 to 13 minutes unless mildly crispy but always pliable.
2. In the meantime, split the bacon's size into pieces of cucumbers, broccoli, and avocado.
3. Spread an equal surface of cream cheese from each strip until the bacon is cold enough to touch it. Divide the vegetables into the bacon equally and put them in one hand. Strictly roll up the vegetables.
4. Season with and serve the sesame seeds.

Keto Chicken Parmesan

TOTAL TIME: 0 HOURS 55 MINS

YIELDS: 4

INGREDIENTS:

- 4 boneless without skin breasts of chicken
- Kosher salt
- 1c. of Almond Flour
- 3 big, beaten eggs
- 3 c. of Parmesan, freshly grated, and much more for serving
- 2 Tsp. of Powdered garlic
- 1 1/2 c. of Mozzarella Sliced
- 1 Tsp. of onion in powdered form
- 2 Tsp. of Oregano dried
- Oil for vegetables
- 3/4 c. Sugar-free, low-carb tomato sauce
- Fresh leaves of basil for topping

DIRECTIONS

1. Preheat the oven to 400 degrees. Halve the chicken breasts crosswise with a sharp knife. Season the chicken with salt and pepper on both sides.
2. Put the almond flour and eggs in 2 different shallow cups. Combine the parmesan, garlic (powder), onion (powder), and oregano in the third shallow dish. With salt and pepper, season.
3. Dip the chicken cutlets into the almond flour, then the eggs, the Parmesan mixture, and push to cover.
4. Heat 2 teaspoons of oil in a large skillet. Add chicken and roast, 2 to 3 minutes on each hand, until golden and cooked through. Function as required in batches, inserting more oil as appropriate.

5. Move the fried cutlets to a 9-inch-x-13-inch baking dish, distribute the tomato sauce uniformly over each cutlet, and finish with the mozzarella.
6. Bake for 10 to 12 minutes before the cheese melts. If needed, broil for 3 minutes until the cheese is golden.
7. Until eating, top with basil and more Parmesan.

Tuscan Butter Shrimp

TOTAL TIME: 0 HOURS 55 MINS

YIELDS: 4

INGREDIENTS

- 2 tbsp. of olive oil extra-virgin
- 1 lb. deveined, peeled, lobster and tails cut
- salt (kosher)
- Black pepper freshly roasted
- 3 tbsp. of Butter
- 3 garlic cloves, minced
- 1 1/2 c. of halved tomatoes with cherry
- 3 c. of spinach for kids
- 1/2 c. of heavy cream
- 1/4 c. of Parmesan, finely grated
- 1/4 c. of thinly cut basil
- Lemon wedges meant for serving as an option

DIRECTIONS

1. Heat oil in a frying pan over medium heat. Season the shrimp with salt and pepper all over. Add the shrimp and sear until the underside is golden, around 2 minutes, and then turn until opaque, until the oil is shimmering but still not burning. Remove and set aside from the skillet.
2. Lower the heat to mild and add some butter. When the butter is melted, stir in the garlic and simmer for around 1 minute, until fragrant. Sprinkle with salt and

substitute the cherry tomatoes. Cook until the tomatoes start to burst, then add the spinach and cook until the spinach begins to wilt.

3. Stir in the heavy cream, basil and parmesan cheese and carry the mixture to a boil. Reduce the heat to low and boil for around 3 minutes before the sauce is significantly reduced.

4. Place the shrimp back in the pan and mix to blend. Cook unless shrimp is cooked through, garnish with more basil, and squeeze lemon on top before eating.

Zoodle Alfredo with Bacon

TOTAL TIME: 0 HOURS 20 MINS

YIELDS: 4

INGREDIENTS:

- 1/2 lb. of Chopped bacon
- 1 minced shallot,
- 2 garlic cloves, minced
- 1/4 c. of Black Alcohol, White Wine
- 1 1/2 c. of heavy cream
- 1/2 c. of Parmesan(cheese) grated, but mostly for garnishing
- 1 pack of zucchini (noodles) (16 oz.)
- Kosher Salt
- Black pepper freshly roast

DIRECTIONS

1. Cook the bacon until crisp, 8 minutes, in a wide saucepan over medium heat. Drain it on a tray lined with paper towels.

2. Pour all but 2 teaspoons of (bacon); then shallots are included. Cook until tender, around 2 minutes, and then add garlic and cook for about 30 seconds until it is fragrant. Add wine and cook before half the quantity is depleted.

3. Connect the heavy cream to the mixture and get it to a boil. Lower the flame and stir in the Parmesan cheese. Cook for about 2 minutes, until the sauce, has thick

somewhat. Add the zucchini (noodles) and toss in the sauce until thoroughly covered. Take the heat off and stir in the fried bacon.

Keto Chicken Soup

TOTAL TIME: 1 HOUR 0 MINS

YIELDS: 4 - 6

INGREDIENTS:

- 2 tbsp. Oil for vegetables
- 1 medium onion, minced
- 5 garlic cloves, crushed
- 2" Fresh ginger bit, sliced
- 1 tiny cauliflower, sliced into florets
- 3/4 Tsp. smashed flakes of red pepper
- 1 medium carrot, on a bias, peeled and thin slices
- 6 c. low-sodium broth of poultry
- 1 celery stem, thinly sliced
- 2 skinless, boneless breasts of chicken
- For garnish, finely cut parsley

DIRECTIONS

1. Heat oil in a big pot over low heat. Add the carrot, ginger, and garlic. Cook before the browning stops.
2. In the meantime, pulse cauliflower before it is split into rice-sized granules in a food processor. Return the cauliflower to the pot with the onion mixture and cook for around 8 minutes over medium-high heat until golden.
3. Bring to a boil and incorporate pepper flakes, onions, celery and chicken (broth). Add the chicken breasts and cook gently for around 15 minutes before they hit a temp of 165 ° C. Remove from the pan, leave to cool and shred until cool enough

to treat. Meanwhile, proceed to cook, 3 to 5 minutes more, until the vegetables are soft.

4. Apply the (Shredded) chicken back to the broth and cut the ginger from the bath. Season with salt and pepper to taste, then garnish before serving with parsley.

Foil Pack Grilled Salmon with Lemony Asparagus

TOTAL TIME: 0 HOURS **20** MINS

YIELDS: 4

INGREDIENTS:

- 20 spears of asparagus, cut
- 4 6-oz. Skin-on fillets of salmon
- 4Tbsp. of Butter, break
- 2 lemons, cut
- Kosher salt
- Black pepper freshly roasted
- Broken dill (fresh), for season

DIRECTIONS:

1. On a hard floor lie two bits of foil. Put on the foil five spears of asparagus and finish with a salmon fillet, 1 tablespoon of butter, and two lemon slices. Cover loosely, and repeat for the rest of the ingredients and you'll have a limit of four sets.
2. High Heat Barbecue. To fry and barbecue, apply foil packets until salmon is cook through and asparagus is soft for about 10 minutes.
3. Sprinkle and mix with dill.

Garlicky Shrimp Zucchini Pasta

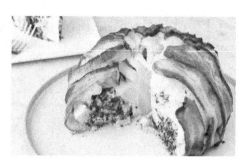

TOTAL TIME: 1 HOUR 50 MINS

YIELDS: 4

INGREDIENTS

- 1/4 c. Of olive oil extra-virgin
- 1/4 c. the Juice in Lemons
- Kosher (salt)
- 1 head (cauliflower), cut leaves and trimmed stem such that cauliflower lies flat but still intact
- 1 (10-oz.) box of frozen (spinach), thawed, stretched out and sliced with water
- 2 big, beaten eggs
- 4 green onions, cut thinly
  - 2 cloves of garlic, minced
  - 3/4 c. of cheddar Shredded
  - 4 oz. of soft and cube white cheese
  - 1/2 c. panko a panko
  - 1/4 c. of parmesan Rubbed
  - 1 lb. of bacon thinly cut

DIRECTIONS

1. Preheat the oven to 450 degrees. In a big kettle, put eight cups of water, oil, lemon juice and 2 tablespoons of salt to a boil. Add the cauliflower and get it to a simmer again. To hold it submerged, reduce it to a gentle simmer and put a plate on top of the cauliflower. Simmer for around 12 minutes before a knife is quickly inserted into the middle.
2. Transfer the cauliflower to a narrow rimmed baking sheet using 2 slotted spoons or a mesh spider. Only let it cool.
3. In the meanwhile, add lettuce (eggs, green onions, garlic, cheddar, cream cheese, panko, and parmesan cheese) and placed a 3/4-inch tip in a piping bag.
4. Place on a rimmed baking sheet with cooled cauliflower stem side up. Pipe filling of florets between stalks. Flip down the side of the cauliflower stem, and then

spread bacon strips, only slightly overlapping strips, over the cauliflower, tucking strip ends into the cauliflower bottom.

5. Roast, halfway through the spinning pan, before golden all over, maybe 30 minutes.

Cajun Parmesan Salmon

TOTAL TIME: 0 HOURS 45 MINS

YIELDS: 4

INGREDIENTS:

- 1 tbsp. Olive oil (extra-virgin)
- 4 (4-oz.) Salmon fillets (preferably wild)
- 2 Tsp. Seasoning the Cajun
- 2 Tbsp. of Butter
- 3 garlic cloves, minced
- 1/3 c. Low-sodium(chicken) or soup with vegetables
- Juice of 1 lemon
- 1 Tbsp. of honey
- 1 Tbsp. Freshly sliced parsley, with more for garnishing
- 2Tbsp. Parmesan, finely chopped
- Slices of lemon, for serving

DIRECTIONS

1. Heat oil in a frying pan over medium heat. Season the salmon with 1 tsp. of Cajun pepper and seasoning, then apply the skin-side-up to the skillet. Cook the salmon for around 6 minutes before it is intensely brown, then turn and cook for 2 more minutes. Transfer to a dish.
2. To the skillet, apply butter and garlic. Stir in the Broth, lemon juice, sugar, remaining Cajun seasoning teaspoon (parsley), and parmesan when the butter has melted. Take the combination to a boil.

3. Lower the heat to mild and return the salmon to the skillet. Simmer for 3 or 4 more minutes before the sauce is decreased, and the salmon is fried.
4. Apply slices of lemon to the pan and eat.

Beef Tenderloin:

TOTAL TIME: 1 HOUR **50** MINS

YIELDS: 4

INGREDIENTS

FOR BEEF:

- 1/2 c. Olive oil (extra-virgin)
- 2 Tbsp. Vinegar (Balsamic)
- 2 Tbsp. Mustard, whole grain
- Thyme(fresh), 3 sprigs
- 3 rosemary sprigs, fresh
- 1 bay leaf
- 2 garlic cloves, crushed
- 2 tbsp. of honey
- 1 (2-lb.) tenderloin beef
- 1 Tsp. salt, Kosher
- 1 Tsp. Black pepper, roasted, fresh
- 1 Tsp. The Dried(Rosemary)
- 1 garlic clove, minced

- **SAUCE FOR YOGURT**

- 1/2 c. Yogurt (Greek)
- 1/4 c. Sour milk, sour cream
- 1 Tsp. Horseradish prepared
- 1/2 lemon extract
- Kosher salt

DIRECTIONS

1. Mix the vinegar, oil, thyme, mustard, rosemary, crushed garlic, bay leaf, and honey together in a wide container. Return the meat to the package, cover with plastic wrap, and marinate for 1 hour or up to one day in the refrigerator. Optional: Before frying, get the tenderloin to room temperature.
2. Preheat the oven to around 450C. Line an aluminum foil rimmed baking sheet and fit a wire rack inside. Strip the marinade from the tenderloin and wipe it dry with paper towels. Add salt, pepper, rosemary, and minced garlic to season all over and put on the rack.
3. Roast until baked to your taste, around 20 minutes for special occasions. Until slicing, let it rest for 5 to 10 minutes.
4. Meanwhile, render the sauce: whisk the milk, sour cream, horseradish and lemon juice together in a medium container, and season with salt.
5. Slice the tenderloin and eat it on the side with sauce.

Baked Cajun Salmon

TOTAL TIME: 0 HOURS 30 MINS

YIELDS: 4

INGREDIENTS

- 1/2 large size white onion, cut thinly
- bell pepper (red), cut thinly
- 1 thinly cut orange bell pepper
- cloves of thinly sliced garlic
- Salt (kosher)
- Black Pepper, fresh, ground
- Three Tbsp. of Olive Oil (Extra-Virgin)
- 1 Tbsp. of thyme in dry form
- 1 Tbsp. of seasoning (Cajun)
- 2 Tsp. Of tweet paprika

- Tsp. of powdered garlic
- 6-oz. Filets of Salmon

DIRECTIONS:

1. Preheat the oven to 400 degrees. Stir in the onions, pepper and garlic on a broad baking dish. Season with pepper and salt and toss with gasoline.
2. Prepare a spice mix: mix together thyme, Cajun seasoning, and paprika and garlic powder in a small cup.
3. On a baking sheet, put the salmon, top the bits with the seasoning mixture and rub them all over the salmon.
4. Bake for 20 minutes until the vegetables and salmon are soft and cooked properly.

Chapter 5: Deserts and Snacks Recipes

Keto Sugar-Free Cheesecake

TOTAL TIME: 8 HOURS 0 MINS

YIELDS: 8 - 10

INGREDIENTS:

- 1/2 c. of almond flour
- 1/2 c. Flour of coconut
- 1/4 c. of coconut, shredded
- 1/2 c. (1 stick) of melted butter
- 3 (8-oz.) cream cheese blocks, soft to room temp
- 16 oz. of sour cream (room temperature)
- 1 Tbsp. of stevia
- 2 Tsp. a sample of pure vanilla
- 3 large size eggs, at room temperature
- Strawberries, diced, for serving

DIRECTIONS

1. Heat the oven to 300 degrees. Create the crust: Oil a spring pan of 8 or 9 inches and coat the bottom and sides with foil. Mix the rice, coconut, and butter together in a medium dish. Push the crust towards the bottom and the sides of the prepared pan somewhat upwards. When you prepare the filling, put the pan in the fridge.

2. Prepare the filling: mix together the cream cheese and sour cream in a large bowl, then whisk in the stevia and vanilla. One at a time, add the eggs, combining after each addition. Layer the filling over the crust uniformly.

3. Put the cheesecake in a deep roasting pan and set it on the oven's center rack. Pour sufficient boiling water carefully into the roasting pan to come halfway up the

spring type pan's sides. Bake for 1 hour to 1 hour 20 minutes, until the middle jiggles just slightly. Switch off the oven, but allow the cake to cool steadily for an hour in the oven with the door partially closed.

4. Remove the pan from the boiling water, remove the foil, and then let it cool for at least five hours or overnight in the refrigerator. Slice with the strawberries and garnish.

Keto Chocolate Chip Cookies

TOTAL TIME: 0 HOURS 30 MINS

YIELDS: 18

INGREDIENTS:

- 2 large size eggs
- 1/2 c (1 stick) of butter that has melted
- 2 Tbsp. of heavy milk to heavy cream
- 2 Tsp .pure extract of vanilla
- 2 3/4 c. of almond flour
- 1/4 Tsp. salt, kosher
- 1/4 c. Sugar granulated keto-friendly (such as swerve)
- 3/4 c. Chips of dark chocolate (such as lily's)
- cooking mist

DIRECTIONS

1. Preheat 350° in the oven. Mix the egg with the sugar, vanilla and heavy cream in a big dish. Add the almond flour, salt and swerve to the mixture.
2. Fold in the cookie batter with the chocolate chips. Shape the mixture into 1" balls and arrange 3" apart on baking sheets lined with parchment. Flatten the balls with cooking spray on the bottom of a glass that has been oiled.
3. Bake for around 17 to 19 minutes until the cookies are softly golden.

Keto Chocolate Mug Cake

TOTAL TIME: 0 HOURS 5 MINS

YIELDS: 1

INGREDIENTS:

- 2 Tbsp. of Butter
- 1/4 c. of almond flour
- 2 Tbsp. of powdered cocoa
- 1 large size egg, beaten
- 2 Tbsp. of chocolate chips that are keto-friendly, (such as Lily's)
- 2 Tbsp. of Swerve, Granulated
- 1/2 Tsp. of baking powder
- A pinch of Kosher salt
- For serving, whipped cream (1/4 c.)

DIRECTIONS

1. Put the butter in a microwave-safe mug and heat for 30 seconds before it is melted. Except for whipped cream, add the remaining ingredients and stir until thoroughly mixed. Cook until the cake is set, but always fudgy, for 45 seconds to 1 minute.
2. Serve with whipped cream.

Keto Ice Cream

TOTAL TIME: 8 HOURS 15 MINS

YIELDS: 8

INGREDIENT:

- 2 cans of coconut milk (15-oz.)
- 2 c. of heavy cream
- 1/4 c. Swerve the Sweetener of the Confectioner
- 1 Tsp. of pure vanilla
- A pinch of Kosher salt

DIRECTIONS

1. In the refrigerator, chill the coconut milk for at least 3 hours, preferably overnight.
2. To make whipped coconut: pour coconut cream into a big bowl, keep liquid in the bowl and beat the coconut cream until very smooth using a hand mixer. Only put back.
3. Make the whipped cream: Using a hand mixer in a separate big bowl (or a stand mixer in a bowl), beat heavy cream until soft peaks shape. Beat in the vanilla and sweetener.
4. Fold the whipped (coconut) into the whipped cream, and then add the mixture to the loaf plate.
5. Freeze for about 5 hours until it is firm.

Keto Hot Chocolate

TOTAL TIME: 0 HOURS 10 MINS

YIELDS: 1 CUP

INGREDIENTS:

- 2 Tbsp. Powder of unsweetened chocolate, and more for garnishing
- 2 1/2 Tsp. of sugar that is keto-friendly, such as Swerve
- 1 1/4 c. Aquatic Water
- 1/4 c. Heavy milk to heavy cream
- 1/4 Tsp. of pure vanilla

- Whipped(milk),for serving

DIRECTIONS:

1. Whisk together the swerve, chocolate, and about 2 teaspoons of water in a shallow pan over medium heat until smoother and dissolve. Increases heat to low, add the remaining cream and water and whisk until heated regularly.
2. Attach the vanilla, and spill it into a cup. Represent with (whipped) cream and chocolate powder dusting.

Keto Peanut Butter Cookies

TOTAL TIME: 1 HOUR 30 MINS

YIELDS: 22

INGREDIENTS

- 1 1/2c. of smooth peanut butter, unsweetened, melted (plus more for drizzling)
- 1 c. Flour of coconut
- 1/4 c. Keto-friendly brown sugar packets, such as Swerve
- 1 Tsp. of pure vanilla
- Pinch of Kosher salt
- 2 c. of melted keto-friendly dark chocolate chips, including Lily's,
- 1 Tbsp. of Cream (Coconut)
-

DIRECTIONS

1. Combine the sugar, coconut flour, peanut butter, salt, and vanilla in a medium dish. Until smooth, stir.
2. Line the parchment paper with a baking sheet. Shape the mixture into circles using a small cookie scoop, then push down gently to flatten slightly and position it on the baking sheet. Freeze until strong, roughly 1 hour.
3. Whisk the melting chocolate and coconut oil together in a medium dish.

4. Dip peanut butter rounds in chocolate using a fork until fully covered and then return to the baking sheet. Drizzle with much more peanut butter, and freeze for around 10 minutes before the chocolate is set.

5. Only serve it cold. In the fridge, put some leftovers.

Chocolate Keto Cookies

TOTAL TIME: 0 HOURS 25 MINS

YIELDS: 11

INGREDIENTS

- 2 1/2 Tbsp. of butter
- 3 Tbsp. of chocolate chips with keto, split
- 1large size egg
- 1 Tsp. of pure vanilla
- 2/3 of c. Almond Flour Blanched
- 1/3 c. of swerve Confectioners
- 3 1/2 Tbsp. Unsweetened dark chocolate powder
- 1/2 Tsp. Powder used for baking
- Pinch of Kosher salt

DIRECTIONS

1. Preheat the oven to 325 degrees. Add butter and half of the (chocolate chips) into a medium-sized dish. Microwave for 15 to 30 seconds, only enough time to melt the chocolate and butter mildly. Until a chocolate sauce emerges, mix the two together.
2. Attach and whisk the egg in a tiny dish before the yolk mixes with the whites. When it's finished, add the chocolate syrup to the bowl with the egg and vanilla extract. Again, blend.
3. To finish the cookies, add the majority of the dry ingredients, save some of the chocolate chips. Mix until it shapes a mass of chocolate cookie dough.
4. To make 11 equal-sized cookies, use a cookie spoon (or a tablespoon). Attach the cookie to a baking parchment paper and top the remainder of the chocolate chips with each cookie. In either a spoon or a spatula, flatten each cookie.
5. For 8 to 10 minutes, roast. When they come out of the oven, they should be very soft, but don't worry, this is natural!

6. Let the cookies on the baking sheet cool off. They can set up and firm up while they cool up.
7. When the leftovers are cooled, enjoy them and store them in an airtight jar in the refrigerator.

Walnut Snowball Cookies:

TOTAL TIME: 1 HOUR 5 MINS

YIELDS: 15

INGREDIENTS

- 1/2 c. (1 stick) of butter that has melted
- 1 large size egg
- 50 drops of stevia liquid (about 1/4 tsp.)
- 1/2 tsp. of pure vanilla
- 1 c. With walnuts
- 1/2 c. Flour of coconut, plus 1 or 2 tbsp. For rolling, more
- 1/2 c. of swerve Confectioners

DIRECTIONS

1. Preheat the oven to 300 ° and use parchment paper to cover a baking sheet. In a large bowl, mix the melted butter, egg, vanilla extract, stevia and set aside.
2. In a food processor, add the walnuts and pulse until ground. In a medium bowl, pour the walnut flour and add the coconut flour and 1/4 cup Swerve and press until mixed.
3. Add the dry mixture to the wet in two sections and whisk to blend. The dough should be soft but strong enough at this stage to shape hand-made balls without sticking to your hands. If the quality is not right, add 1 to 2 tablespoons of extra (coconut) flour and mix.
4. Create 15 balls of the same size and place them on a lined baking sheet. In the microwave, they would not disperse.
5. For 30 minutes, roast.

6. Enable 5 minutes to settle, and then in the remaining 1/4 cup Swerve, roll the (still warm) spheres.
7. Put them back on the parchment paper and give another 20 to 30 minutes to cool fully before feeding.

Keto Tortilla Chips

TOTAL TIME: 0 HOURS 35 MINS

YIELDS: 4 - 6

INGREDIENTS

- 2 c. of Mozzarella cheese, Sliced
- 1 c. of almond flour
- 1 Tsp. salt, Kosher
- 1 Tsp. of garlic powder
- 1/2 Tsp. Powdered chili
- Black pepper freshly ground

DIRECTIONS

1. Preheat the oven to 350 degrees. Top the parchment paper with two wide baking sheets.
2. Melt the mozzarella in a secure microwave bowl for around 1 minute and 30 seconds. Add the almond flour, cinnamon, chili powder, garlic powder, black pepper and a few pieces. Use both hands to moisten the dough a couple of times before it forms a smooth shape.
3. Place the dough between two parchment paper sheets and stretch it out into a 1/8' wide rectangle. Break the dough into triangles using a knife or a pizza cutter.
4. Spread the chips on lined baking sheets and bake for 12 to 14 minutes until the sides are golden and begin to crisp.

Keto Burger Fat Bombs

TOTAL TIME: 0 HOURS 30 MINS

YIELDS: 20

INGREDIENTS:

- Cooking mist
- 1 lb. of meat, ground
- 1/2 tsp. powder in garlic form
- salt (kosher)
- Black pepper freshly ground
- 2 tbsp. Cold butter, 20 bits of sliced butter
- 2 oz. Split into 20 bits of cheddar,
- Lettuce berries meant for serving
- For serving, finely sliced tomatoes
- Mustard, to serve

DIRECTIONS

1. Preheat the oven to 375 °C and oil the cooking spray with a mini muffin tin. Season the beef with salt, garlic powder and pepper in a medium dish.
2. Place 1 teaspoon of beef equally, covering the bottom entirely, into the bottom of each muffin tin cup. Place a slice of butter on top and press 1 teaspoon of beef over the butter to cover full.
3. In each cup, place a slice of cheddar on top of the meat and force the remaining beef over the cheese to cover it fully.
4. Bake for about 15 minutes before the meat is ready. Let yourself cool somewhat.
5. Using a metal offset spatula carefully to release each burger out of the tin. Serve with onions, salad leaves, and mustard.

Jalapeño Popper Egg Cups

TOTAL TIME: 0 HOURS 45 MINS

YIELDS: 12

INGREDIENTS:

- 12 strips of bacon
- 10 eggs (large)
- 1/4 c. of sour milk,
- 1/2 c. Cheddar Shredded
- 1/2 c. Mozzarella Sliced
- 2(jalapeños), 1 sliced thinly and 1 finely chopped
- 1 Tsp. Powdered of garlic
- salt(kosher)
- Black pepper freshly ground
- Cooking spray, nonstick

DIRECTIONS

1. Preheat the oven to 375 degrees. Over medium heat, (cook bacon) in a broad skillet until well browned but always pliable. Put aside to drain on a paper towel-lined pan.
2. Whisk the eggs, sour cream, cheese, minced jalapeño and garlic in powder form together in a big bowl. With salt and pepper, season.
3. Oil a muffin tin with the aid of nonstick cooking oil. Line each well with one bacon strip, then pour each muffin cup with egg mixture until around two-thirds of the way through to the end. Cover each muffin with a slice of jalapeño.
4. Bake for 20 minutes until the eggs do not look moist anymore. Before withdrawing them from the muffin pan, cool slightly.

Keto Frosty

TOTAL TIME: 0 HOURS 45 MINS

YIELDS: 4

INGREDIENTS

- 1 1/2 c. Heavy cream whipping
- 2 Tbsp. Unsweetened powder of cocoa
- 3 Tbsp. Sweetener for (keto-friendly) powdered sugar, such as a Swerve
- 1 Tsp. of pure vanilla
- Pinch of Kosher salt

DIRECTIONS

1. Combine the milk, sugar, sweetener, vanilla, and salt in a wide pot. Beat the mixture until rigid peaks shape, and use a hand blender or (the whisk attachment of a stand mixer). Mix the scoops into a Ziploc container and ice for 30 to 35 minutes before they're frozen.
2. Break the tip off an edge of the Ziploc container and pour it into dishes to eat.

Bacon Guac Bombs

TOTAL TIME: 0 HOURS 45 MINS
YIELDS: 15
INGREDIENTS:

2 bacon strips, fried and crumbled

For guacamole

- 2 pitted, sliced, and mashed avocados
- 6 oz. of Cream cheese, cooked, softened
- 1 lime juice
- 1 clove of garlic, minced
- 1/4 of red onion, minced
- 1 small jalapeno (seeded if less fire is preferred), chopped
- 2 Tbsp. Cilantro, freshly sliced
- 1/2 Tsp. of cumin seeds
- 1/2 Tsp. Powdered of chili
- salt(kosher)
- Black pepper freshly ground

DIRECTIONS

1. Combine all the guacamole products in a big bowl. Stir unless mostly smooth, and add salt and pepper (some pieces are OK). Put in the freezer for 30 minutes to firm up rapidly.

2. On a wide tray, put crumbled bacon. Scoop the guacamole mix and put in the bacon, utilizing a little cookie scoop. Roll in the bacon to coat. Repeat before you've used both the bacon and guacamole. Store in refrigerator.

Avocado Chips

TOTAL TIME: 0 HOURS 40 MINS
YIELDS: 15
INGREDIENTS

- 1 large ripe avocado
- 3/4 c. Freshly grated parmesan
- 1 tsp. Lemon juice
- 1/2 tsp. Garlic powder
- 1/2 tsp. Italian seasoning
- Kosher salt

- Freshly ground black pepper

DIRECTIONS

1. Preheat oven to 325° and line two baking sheets with parchment paper. In a medium bowl, mash avocado with a fork until smooth. Stir in parmesan, lemon juice, garlic powder, and Italian seasoning. Season with salt and pepper.
2. Place heaping teaspoon-size scoops of mixture on baking sheet, leaving about 3" apart between each scoop. Flatten each scoop to 3" wide across with the back of a spoon or measuring cup. Bake until crisp and golden, about 30 minutes, then let cool completely. Serve at room temperature.

Rosemary Keto Crackers

TOTAL TIME: 1 HOUR 0 MINS
YIELDS: 140
INGREDIENTS

- 2 1/2 c. almond flour
- 1/2 c. coconut flour
- 1 tsp. ground flaxseed meal
- 1/2 tsp. dried rosemary, chopped
- 1/2 tsp. onion powder
- 1/4 tsp. kosher salt
- 3 large eggs
- 1 tbsp. extra-virgin olive oil

DIRECTIONS

1. Preheat oven to 325° and line a baking sheet with parchment paper. In a large bowl, whisk together flours, flaxmeal, rosemary, onion powder, and salt. Add eggs and oil and mix to combine. Continue mixing until dough forms a large ball, about 1 minute.
2. Sandwich dough between 2 pieces of parchment and roll to ¼" thick. Cut into squares and transfer to prepared baking sheet.
3. Bake until golden, 12 to 15 minutes. Let cool before storing in a resalable container.

Conclusion

A ketogenic diet could be an alternative for certain people who have experienced trouble losing weight with other approaches. The exact ratio of fat, carbohydrate, and protein that is required to attain health benefits can differ among individuals due to their genetic makeup and body structure. Therefore, if one decides to start a ketogenic diet, it is advised to meet with one's physician and a dietitian to closely track any metabolic adjustments since beginning the treatment and to develop a meal schedule that is specific to one's current health problems and to avoid food shortages or other health risks. A dietitian can also have advice on reintroducing carbs after weight reduction is accomplished.

Vegan Keto Meal Plan Cookbook with Pictures

The Low-Fat Plan To Burn Fat, Boost Your Energy, Crush Cravings, And Calm Inflammation

By

Jamie Carter

Table of Contents

Introduction

The Ketogenic diet is a low-carb, high-fat, moderate-protein diet marketed for its effective influence on weight loss and general health.

While sometimes connected with animal foods, this form of consumption may be modified to suit plant-based diet plans, like the vegan diet.

All animal products are excluded from vegan diets, rendering low-carb consumption more complicated. However, vegans will enjoy the possible advantages of a Ketogenic diet with proper preparation.

What is the Keto vegan diet?

The Ketogenic diet has a high-fat content, low carbohydrate content, and mild protein content. In order to achieve and sustain ketosis, carbohydrates are usually limited to 20g to 50g a day. Ketosis is a metabolic mechanism in which the body will burn fat for energy instead of glucose.

Because this form of eating contains mainly fat, typically around 75% of the intake, keto dieters also switch to high-fat animal items, such as butter, pork, chicken beef, and all-dairy products.

Many who consume diets focused on vegetables, like vegans, can also adopt a ketogenic diet. Vegan people only eat plant-based products such as fruit, vegetables, and cereals, while avoiding poultry, meat, milk and eggs from animals. By depending on high-fat, plant-based items such as coconut oil, avocados, seeds and nuts, vegans can achieve ketosis.

Vegan Keto Diet Benefits

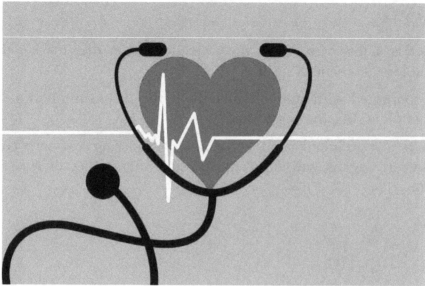

A Vegan Keto diet promises a wide variety of health advantages. A high-fat diet and low-carb are used in the Ketogenic diet. Pairing it with a purely vegan diet allows reduced consumption of carbs and sugar and enhances the absorption of nutrients, which inevitably contributes to outstanding long-term wellbeing. Vegans can achieve ketosis by eating plant-based goods high in healthy fats such as avocados, almonds, seeds, olives and nuts.

So what precisely are the effects of a vegan keto diet for health? How can your physical wellbeing benefit from following this diet?

1. Reduces the likelihood of heart disease

Heart disease is particularly the main culprit of so many deaths globally. Many health problems may cause it, but it is mostly attributed to poor diet, absence of exercise, and obesity.

Many individuals believe that the heart cannot stay healthy with a high-fat diet. But latest findings have shown that healthy fat consumption is safe and offers long-term medical benefits. A regular Vegan Keto diet doesn't really display any substantial rise in cardiac consequences, but it even decreases the extent of heart disease-related fat molecules, triglycerides, flowing in your blood circulation.

2. Preventing and Treating Diabetes and Obesity

The ketogenic diet is a successful way to decrease medication in patients with diabetes, based on research. Because the keto-vegan diet decreases the consumption of carbs and guarantees a diet free of sugar, it reduces sugar levels, which greatly reduces the likelihood of potential diabetes. For the people who have diabetes already, this diet enables them to reduce insulin doses or totally eliminates the drugs in as little as a few weeks. In fact, eating a plant-based diet that is sugar-free and low-carb is an efficient way to lose and manage the target weight.3.

3. Battles some kinds of cancer

Most evidence reveals that sugar fuels cancer cells. Keto-vegan food removes sugar from the system. Your system's reduction in sugars and nutrients starves the cancer cells. A relatively low-carbohydrate diet, for example, can decrease the relapse of some forms of breast cancer. It has even been shown to slow down brain tumor development. Cancerous cells can be deliberately starved by reducing the intake of sugary fruits and starchy vegetables. Many Keto-vegan products help inhibit the growth of cancer cells.

4. Enhances mental health

Researchers believe that a healthy Keto-vegan diet increases mental cognition, strengthening your critical reasoning ability and making you more concentrated. This lifestyle leaves the brain sharp and fresh.

The keto-vegan diet also aims to clear up beta-amyloid cholesterol, which can bind together to block signals from flowing quickly and efficiently in the brain. Preventing this build-up implies reducing the risk of contracting neurodegenerative disorders such as Alzheimer's.

5. Provides good health for the gut and stomach

Having keto-vegan foods in your diet helps your gut to be healthy with a diverse and balanced intestinal microbiome. A strong gut with lots of beneficial bacteria allows the body to consume nutrients and fats more easily and more safely. These healthy bacteria benefit you by having a strong lining of the intestine that helps break down your food and promotes the absorption of nutrients. Some bacteria in the intestine also help to supply your body with vitamins B12 and potassium that are necessary for regulating minerals such as calcium in your body. Besides, this diet makes sure the metabolism is balanced.

6. Helps to improve eye and vision

It is possible to avoid glaucoma and cataracts, chronic conditions that cause blurred vision or perhaps even blindness, with a keto-vegan lifestyle. Getting a diet that is low in carbs but high in healthy fats will improve the health of the retinal cells and reduce cell degeneration as well.

7. Hormones Stabilizes

In the body, hormones are molecular messengers. There may be chaotic hormonal imbalances. Ketosis has a positive effect on hormones. It reduces the body's insulin levels by eliminating sugar from the diet. Other than that, leptin levels, a form of hormones that suppresses appetite, are lowered, allowing you to manage your eating behaviors.

In women following the Keto-vegan diet, their pituitary gland performs much better, controlling progesterone and thyroid to reduce infertility and progesterone deficiency.

8. Clearer and cleaner skin

In your system, reducing carbohydrates results in cleaner skin. Simple carbs and dairy products can also cause inflammation, which is one of the main causes of acne.

High-glycemic food can make acne worse and also cause breakouts. Although sugar and carbohydrates are known to induce pimples, healthy fats can alleviate dry skin and inhibit inflammatory acne from occurring. So, if you desire your skin to be smoother, clearer and brighter, this diet is the answer.

9. Provides greater amounts of vitality to assist you in getting around during the day

Increased carb consumption makes you feel sluggish. The starches found in the foods are converted into glucose as you eat food rich in carbohydrates (pizza, for example). There would be an increase in energy after eating extra carbs, but a major decline will come immediately, leaving you to feel slow and exhausted after having a meal.

You will face none of these difficulties on a Keto vegan diet. Instead of carbs, your body would then depend on fats. It would not need energy from carbohydrates. Increased insulin production can be stopped, and at any moment, the body will now use fat reserves. You will experience a steady supply of energy during the day with this.

10. Helps improve sleep

Also, it enhances sleep. The best thing about complying with this plan's that it lets you stay up and about in the daytime and gives you a satisfying, nice night's sleep.

Sleep cycles change thanks to a decrease in carbohydrates and a rise in healthy fats. Researchers believe that a vegan- keto diet could influence the development of a chemical in the brain, adenosine, which controls sleep.

Besides weight loss, the Vegan-keto diet has so many health benefits. It would be a long list if we started to mention them all in here. Try a keto-vegan program now and enjoy all the wellness benefits that it will bring!

Foods to avoid on a vegan keto diet

When ensuing to a keto vegan diet, you must considerably decrease your carb consumption and substitute carbs with healthy fats and vegan protein sources.to

Animal products, including meat, poultry, dairy eggs, and seafood, are omitted from a keto vegan diet.

These are some of the foods that must be completely shunned:

Seafood: Fish, clams, shrimp, mussels.

Meat and poultry: Turkey, chicken, pork beef.

Eggs: Egg whites and yolks.

Animal-based products: Honey, whey protein, egg white protein.

Dairy: Milk, yogurt, butter.

These foods ought to be considerably reduced:

Sugary drinks: Soda, juice, sweet tea, sports drinks, chocolate milk smoothies.

Alcoholic beverages, high in carbs, wine, sweetened cocktails, beer.

Diet foods Low in fat: Low-fat products tend to be elevated in added sugar.

Grains and starches: Cereal, bread, baked goods, rice, grains, pasta.

Legumes and Beans: Red kidney beans, black and white chickpeas and black beans.

Sweeteners: Maple syrup, white sugar, Brown sugar, agave.

Starchy vegetables: Sweet potatoes, winter squash, potatoes, peas beets.

Fruits: Limit all fruit intake. Nevertheless, few fruits like different berries are permitted in small portions.

Processed foods: Restrain from packaged foods and encourage consumption of whole, unrefined foods.

High-carb sauces and condiments: Marinades, sweetened salad dressings, Barbecue sauce,

The degree of carbohydrate limitation when doing a keto vegan plan differs depending upon the individual's requirements and health objectives.

In general, vegan protein sources and Good, high-fat vegan foods should be prevalent in your diet.

Foods to consume on a keto vegan diet

Following a healthy keto vegan diet requires that the vegan meals be made of low-carb and high-fat.

In the keto vegan diet, some permissible foods are:

Oils: MCT oil, olive oil, coconut oil, nut oil, avocado oil.

Coconut produces: Unsweetened coconut (flakes or shredded), coconut cream, Full-fat coconut milk.

Non-starchy veggies: Brussels sprouts, zucchini Leafy greens, broccoli, cauliflower, mushrooms peppers.

Nuts and seeds: Hemp seeds, walnuts, almonds, Brazil nuts, macadamia nuts, pumpkin seeds, chia seeds.

Seed and nut butter: Butters from sunflower seeds, almonds, cashews, peanuts.

Vegan "dairy": Vegan cream cheese, full-fat coconut yogurt, vegan butter, cashew cheese.

Vegan sources of protein: Tempeh, tofu (full-fat).

Berries: Raspberries Blueberries, strawberries and blackberries, can be consumed in control.

Avocados: Guacamole Whole avocados.

Condiments: Fresh herbs, spices, nutritional yeast, lemon juice, pepper, salt,

Since the keto diet leaves out several of the food types that vegans depend on, such as starchy veggies and whole grains, the keto vegan diet can indeed be adopted adequately.

Drawbacks and side effects

Although the vegan keto diet may be helpful to your wellbeing, it has some possible drawbacks.

Downsides

Keto vegan diets appear to be low in essential nutrients, — particularly if not carefully prepared. Vitamin D, vitamin K2, vitamin B12, omega-3 fats, zinc, iron and calcium, are some of the nutrients deficient in some vegan diets.

The Vegan Keto diet has more limitations than any normal vegan diet; that's why it is necessary to be fortified with high-quality vitamins and minerals. The meals you prepare should guarantee that you are consuming a nutritionally balanced diet.

Consuming fortified foods, concentrating on whole foods, and consuming nutrients, such as fermentation and sprouts, is vital for individuals adopting a vegan keto diet.

However, it can be difficult for individuals on the vegan keto diet to fulfill their micro-nutrient needs with the vegan or keto foods alone. Supplementing some minerals and vitamins that are typically deficient in vegan diets is a clever way to reduce future shortages and guarantee that your everyday requirements are fulfilled.

Adverse Effects

It may be daunting to switch to a ketogenic diet.

Sometimes termed keto flu, the body may find it difficult to move from a higher carbohydrate diet to a keto diet.

When your body changes from using glucose to fat for energy, painful symptoms can occur.

Adverse effects of vegan keto diets may include:

- Headaches
- Diarrhea
- Fatigue
- Irritability
- Nausea
- Poor concentration

- Muscle cramps
- Weakness
- Difficulty sleeping
- Constipation
- Dizziness

Drinking plenty of water, having adequate rest, consuming fiber-rich meals and participating in moderate exercise will help relieve keto-flu effects.

Also, potassium, magnesium, and sodium electrolyte supplementation may help alleviate some effects, such as muscle pain, fatigue and insomnia.

Since the vegan keto diet limits certain items, it is not appropriate for all.

A vegan keto diet might not be appropriate for people with diabetes, type 1 ladies who are breast-feeding or are pregnant, sports professionals or those with a history of disordered eating.

When you are considering a transition to a keto vegan diet, contact a doctor or a licensed health provider first to confirm that your diet is healthy to adopt.

Chapter 1- Breakfast

1. Vegan Scrambled Eggs

Prep. Time: 10 minutes

Cook Time: 10 minutes

Servings: 4

Serving size: ¼ of the recipe

Nutrition as per serving

182 kcal/ 11g fat / 8g carbs / 14g protein / 2g fiber = 6g net carbs

Ingredients

- Silken tofu 300 g
- Plant-based milk, unsweetened ½ cup
- Nutritional yeast 2 tbsp.
- Almond flour 2 tbsp.
- Ground turmeric heaped ¼ tsp.
- Dijon mustard 1 tsp.
- Cornstarch or cornflour 2 tsp.
- Indian black salt 1 tsp.+ more to taste
- Fine salt ½ tsp. + more to taste
- Black pepper ½ tsp. + more to taste
- Onion powder ½ tsp.
- Garlic powder ½ tsp.
- Vegan butter 2 tbsp.
- Extra-firm or firm tofu 350 g (for crumbling effect to get eggy texture)

Directions

1. In a blender, add the milk, silken tofu, nutritional yeast, turmeric, almond flour, mustard, pepper, cornstarch, black salt, salt, garlic powder, onion powder, and blend absolutely smooth.
2. Crush the other chunk of tofu, either with fingers or use a potato masher.
3. In a large frypan, melt the vegan butter over a medium-low flame. When it melts, add the crushed tofu. Cook it for a couple of minutes, then add in the smoothly blended tofu mixture. Stir and continue occasionally stirring until the desired texture is reached for about 5 minutes. It should be slightly runny and silky. It will get drier if you cook longer. Once you take it off the heat, it will keep cooking a little so keep that in mind.
4. When ready, taste the seasoning and add black salt, salt, and pepper if necessary and serve immediately.

2. Avocado & Vegan Bulletproof Coffee

Prep. Time: 5 minutes

Servings: 1

Serving size 1 vegan Bpc + half avocado

Nutrition as per serving

255 kcal / 26g fat / 7g carbs / 1g protein /5g fiber = 2g net carb

Ingredients

- Coffee 1 cup
- Cinnamon a pinch
- MCT oil 1 tbsp.
- Avocado ½
- For Everything Bagel Seasoning:
- White sesame seeds 2 tbsp.
- Garlic dried minced 1 tbsp.
- Coarse sea salt, 1 tbsp.
- Poppy seeds 1 tbsp.
- Onion dried minced 1 tbsp.
- Black sesame seeds 1 tbsp.

Directions

1. Add MCT oil, brewed coffee, and cinnamon in a blender, process until frothy, then transfer to a coffee mug to serve.
2. Mix all seasoning ingredients in a bowl.
3. Cut avocado into half, remove skin and slice as preferred.
4. Sprinkle the prepared seasoning. Serve!

3. Overnight Vegan Keto Chia Pudding

Prep. Time: 10 minutes

Resting time: 6 hours

Servings: 1

Serving size: 1 bowl

Nutrition as per serving

151 kcal / 10g fat / 12.5g carbs / 11g fiber / 5g protein = 1.5g net carbs

Ingredients

For the keto chia pudding

- Plant-based milk (e.g., almond, coconut, or macadamia)1 cup
- Chia seeds, 3 tbsp.
- Keto liquid sweetener (e.g., vanilla stevia drops.) To taste
- Preferred toppings -optional

Directions

1. Add chia seeds to the milk mixing thoroughly, cover and chill in the refrigerator overnight.
2. If it is not of desired consistency, add more liquid. Add keto Sweetener to taste and sprinkle desired toppings and serve.

3. Store in a sealed container in the refrigerator for up to 5 days (i.e., it's perfect for meal prepping!).

4. Low Carb Keto Oatmeal

Prep. Time: 1 minute

Cook Time: 4 minute

Servings: 1 serving

Serving size: 1 bowl

Nutrition as per serving

250kcal / 17g fat /16g carbs / 15g fiber / 8g protein = 1g net carbs

Ingredients

- Coconut milk, unsweetened, cold 1/2 cup
- Water, hot 1/2 cup
- 2 tbsp. each of
- Unsweetened shredded coconut
- Ground flaxseed
- Granulated sweetener, keto-friendly
- Chia seeds

Directions

1. Add the dry ingredients to a small mixing container, and mix well.
2. Pour the hot water into the dry ingredients and mix well; it will turn out super thick. Pour in the cold coconut milk and whisk until it becomes creamy and thick 'oatmeal.'
3. Sprinkle mix-ins or toppings of choice and serve.

5. Tofu Shakshuka

Prep. Time: 5 minutes

Cook Time: 20 minutes

Servings: 2

Serving size: Half the recipe

Nutrition as per serving

284kcal / 9.4g fat / 26.6g carbs / 9.2g fiber / 20.3g protein = 16 net carbs

Ingredients

- Olive oil 1 tablespoon (optional)
- Garlic 4 large cloves
- Tomatoes diced 1 can (750 ml)
- Salt 1 tsp.
- Pepper ½ tsp.
- Dried mixed herbs (or oregano or Italian seasoning) 2 tsp.
- Dried chili flakes 1/2 tsp.
- Medium tofu, unpressed, cut into rounds 1 block (approx.350g)
- Indian black salt optional

Directions

1. In a skillet, heat the olive oil and sauté the garlic on medium heat until it starts to brown a little. (For an oil-free recipe: use a tbsp. of water as a replacement for the oil).
2. Include the tomatoes, pepper, salt, herbs, and chili flakes.
3. Simmer for 5 minutes on medium heat, then put in the tofu rounds.
4. Decrease the heat and simmer on medium-low for 15 minutes till the tofu is soft, and the sauce starts to thicken up a little and thoroughly heated.
5. Add Indian Black Salt just before serving.
6. Serve with keto toast, if your macros allow!

6. Vegan Keto Protein Smoothie Bowl

Prep. Time: 5 minutes

Servings: 1

Serving size: 1 smoothie bowl

Nutrition as per serving

615 kcal / 54g fat / 19g carbs / 13g fiber / 23g protein = 6g net carbs

Ingredients

For Green Smoothie Bowl:

- Spinach 1 cup
- Almond milk unsweetened 2–3 Tbsp.
- Avocado ½
- Macadamia nut butter 1 Tbsp.
- Plain almond milk yogurt, unsweetened ⅔ cup
- Keto sweetener, to taste
- Spirulina powder 2 tsp.

For Toppings:

- Hemp hearts 1 Tbsp.
- Pumpkin seeds 2 Tbsp.
- Chia seeds 1 Tbsp.

Directions

1. Place all the smoothie ingredients (excluding toppings) into a blender and mix until smooth. Add sweetener to taste, altering thickness to preference.
2. Transfer to a bowl, sprinkle on the toppings, and serve!

For meal prep:

1. Keep avocado, spinach, spirulina and nut butter in a freezer-safe bag or jar and freeze.
2. To prepare, before placing in the blender, thaw slightly add milk and yogurt.
3. Blend, pour in a bowl serve with toppings!

7. Cauliflower and Greens Smoothie Bowl

Prep. Time: 5 minutes

Cook Time: 10 minutes

Servings: 2

Serving size: 1 bowl w/o toppings

Nutrition as per serving

253kcal / 14.8g fat / 18.5g carbs / 7g fiber / 12g protein = 4.2g net carbs

Ingredients

- Cauliflower, frozen 1/2 cup
- Zucchini, frozen 1/2 cup
- Spinach (or kale, for calcium boost), frozen loosely packed1 cup
- Blueberries or blackberries, frozen 1 cup
- Milk alternate 1 cup (try almond-milk or hemp milk or canned coconut milk)
- Peanut butter (or almond butter) 2 tbsp.
- Hemp hearts 3 tbsp.
- Cinnamon ground 1 tsp

Toppings- Optional

- Granola (grain-free for low-carb)
- Berries frozen or fresh
- Hemp hearts

Directions

This recipe goes well with frozen zucchini and cauliflower. Cauliflower can be steamed first, but when using a high-speed blender, it will not be necessary. Frozen spinach as well as fresh works fine.

1. In a high-speed blender, put in all the smoothie ingredients, place the frozen ingredients first. Blend until a smooth consistency is reached and all is well incorporated.
2. Split this banana-free smoothie mixture into two soup bowls. Garnish with additional hemp hearts and homemade granola.

8. Maple Low Carb Oatmeal

Prep. Time: 5 minutes

Cook Time: 20 minutes

Servings: 4 servings

Serving size 1 cup

Nutrition as per serving

374kcal / 34.59g fat /28g carbs / 24.7g fiber / 9.25g protein = 3.27g net carbs

Ingredients

- Unsweetened almond milk 4 cups
- Walnuts 1/2 cups
- Sunflower seeds 1/4 cups
- Pecans 1/2 cups
- Coconut flakes 1/4 cup
- Chia seeds 4 tbsp.
- Stevia powder 3/8 tsp
- Cinnamon 1/2 tsp
- Maple flavoring 1 tsp (optional)

Directions

1. In a food processor, place the pecans, walnuts, sunflower seeds, and pulse to have them coarsely chopped.
2. Place all the ingredients in a large saucepan and heat on low. Keep simmering for about 20 to 30 minutes, occasionally stirring, until most of the liquid has been absorbed by the chia seeds. Keep stirring, so the seeds don't stick to the saucepan at the bottom.
3. Once the oatmeal thickens, take off from heat and serve while hot. It can also be cooled down and stored in the refrigerator for the next day's breakfast.

Chapter 2- Lunch

1. Low Carb Vegan Tahini Bowl

Prep. Time: 10 minutes

Cook Time: 35 minutes

Servings: 1

Serving size: 1 bowl

Nutrition as per serving

641 Kcal / 5g fat / 33g carbs / 20g fiber / 23g protein = 13g net carbs

Ingredients

For Vegetable Bowl:

- Brussels sprouts 1 cup
- Broccoli florets 1½ cups
- Tahini 2 Tbsp.
- Pumpkin seeds 2 Tbsp.
- Kalamata olives 10
- Oil ½ tsp
- Salt a pinch
- Avocado, ½ for serving
- Sesame seeds sprinkle for topping

Directions

1. Heat the oven to 220°C (425°F).
2. Line a pan with foil or parchment and add Brussels sprouts, broccoli, and pumpkin seeds. Add tahini, oil, salt and mix.

3. Roast for 35 minutes.
4. Take out from the oven, place Kalamata olives to veggies in the pan, and toss to mix.
5. Transfer to a bowl top with half sliced avocado, then sprinkle some sesame seeds!

2. Easy Low Carb Creamy Spinach

Prep. Time: 5 minutes

Cook Time: 10 minutes

Servings: 4

Serving size: 1/2 cup

Nutrition as per serving

274kcal / 27g fat / 5 g carbs / 1g fiber / 4g protein = 4 net carbs

Ingredients

- Butter 3 tbsp.
- Baby spinach chopped 16 cups (10 oz.)
- Cream cheese, chopped 3 oz.
- Heavy cream 1/2 cup
- Italian seasoning1 tsp.
- Garlic, minced 4 cloves
- Black pepper 1/4 tsp.
- Sea salt 1/4 tsp.
- Parmesan cheese, for topping (optional)

Directions

1. In a large wok or a sauté pan, heat butter over medium heat. Add in minced garlic and fry until fragrant.
2. Include spinach. Fry for 3 to 5 minutes until wilted. Cover the pan if it is too full of stirring at first. Covering it for a few minutes will wilt the spinach quickly. Then cook, stirring until the spinach is almost dry.
3. Add cream cheese, heavy cream, Italian seasoning, black pepper, and sea salt. Stir continuously until the cheese has melted, then cook for 3-4 minutes until thickened.
4. If preferred, sprinkle with Parmesan cheese before serving.

3. Mashed Cauliflower with Garlic and Herbs

Prep. Time: 10 minutes

Cook Time: 10 minutes

Servings: 4

Serving size: ¼ of the recipe

Nutrition as per serving

84.6kcal / 4g fat / 10.9g carbs / 4g fiber / 4.1g protein = 6.9g net carbs

Ingredients

- Cauliflower 1 head
- Olive oil 1 tbsp.
- Garlic, minced 2 cloves
- Herbs chopped finely (rosemary, thyme, parsley, sage, chives, etc.) 1-2 tsp

Directions

1. Trim off the leaves from the cauliflower and remove the florets. Wash the florets.
2. In a pot, heat water (about 1-inch) on medium heat. When the water started boiling, place a steamer insert inside the pot and placed the cauliflower florets in it. Steam for about 6-8 minutes.
3. In the meantime, take a small pan and heat the olive oil on medium heat. Put in the minced garlic, then cook for 30 seconds, and take off the heat.
4. Take out the steamer insert, discard the water, and then add the steamed cauliflower back into the pot. Add the garlic, olive oil, and chopped herbs.
5. Use a stick blender or a potato to gently mix all the ingredients with the cauliflower, do not puree. Serve immediately.

4. Keto Mac and Cheese with Vegan Cheese Sauce

Prep. Time: 5 minutes

Cook Time: 20 minutes

Servings: 4

Serving size: 1 cup

Nutrition as per serving

294kcal / 23g fat / 12g carbs / 5g fiber / 11g protein = 7g net carbs

Ingredients

- Cauliflower (cut into small florets) 1 head
- Butter 2 tbsp. + 1 tbsp.
- Sea salt
- Black pepper
- For the cheese sauce
- Hemp seeds hulled 1 cup
- Nutritional yeast 1/2 cup
- Bell pepper chopped (red, orange or yellow) 1/4 cup
- Salt 1 tsp.
- Onion Powder 1/2 tsp.
- Garlic powder 1/2 tsp.
- water ½ -1 cup

Directions

1. Heat the oven to 232 degrees c (450 degrees f). Line foil or parchment paper on a baking tray.
2. Melt 2 tbsp. of butter in the microwave. In a large mixing bowl, mix the cauliflower florets and the melted butter together. Add black pepper and sea salt to taste.

3. Assemble the seasoned cauliflower florets on the lined baking tray. Bake for about 10 to 15 minutes, or until crispy and tender.
4. Prepare the sauce: Put all ingredients in a blender with half a cup of water in at first and blend until smooth for about 2 minutes. Then gradually add the rest until a thick cheesy consistency is reached. You may need less quantity of water!
5. Mix the cauliflower in the cheese sauce and bake for about 20 minutes just before serving.

5. Indian Masala Whole Roasted Cauliflower in Instant Pot

Prep. Time: 5 minutes

Cook Time: 5 minutes

Servings: 8 servings

Serving size: 1/8 of the recipe

Nutrition as per serving

161 kcal / 10g fat / 16g carbs / 6g fiber / 5g protein = 10g net carbs

Ingredients

- Cauliflower 1 whole head
- Onions, diced 2 large
- Tomatoes, diced 5
- Cashews, ½ cup (soaked in almond milk ½ cup)
- Ginger chopped 1 tsp
- Garlic chopped 1 tsp
- Oil 2 tbsp.
- Cumin seeds ½ tsp
- Black cardamoms 2
- Green cardamom 1
- Cloves 3
- Peppercorn 4
- Bay leaf 1
- Turmeric powder ½ tsp
- Coriander powder 1 tsp
- Red chilly powder 1 tsp (optional)
- Garam masala ½ tsp
- Cilantro, chopped 1 tbsp.
- Roasted sesame seeds 1 tsp (optional)
- Water 2 cups
- Salt to taste

Directions

1. Heat the Instant Pot mode to "Sauté." Put in oil, cloves, cumin seeds, black cardamoms, peppercorns, bay leaf and green cardamom. Stir.

2. Include onions, garlic, ginger and salt. Cook till onions are transparent.
3. At this point, add in the spices, turmeric, chili powder, and coriander powder. Cook for about 2 minutes more, stirring occasionally.
4. Put in the coarsely chopped tomatoes and stir well. Keep cooking until the oil begins to separate. Discard the black cardamoms and bay leaf.
5. In a blender, add cashews and milk, blend slowly, adding hot water. It should be a smooth paste and add it to the instant pot.
6. Now remove the bottom of the cauliflower and wash thoroughly.
7. Add a cup of water and the trivet to the Instant Pot.
8. Position Instant Pot for 00:00 minutes to High "Pressure." Seal the valve. Once the timer is off, move the valve to Vent for Quick release of the pressure.
9. Open the Instant Pot and let the cauliflower cool down a little.
10. Transfer the cauliflower to a serving dish and add half of the sauce.
11. Optional- broil the sauce-covered cauliflower for a few minutes.
12. Sprinkle garam masala cilantro and roasted sesame seeds on top and serve.

6. Low Carb Vegetable Soup

Prep. Time: 5 minutes

Cook Time: 30 minutes

Servings: 12

Serving size: 1 cup

Nutrition as per serving

79kcal / 2g fat / 11g carbs / 3g fiber / 2g protein = 8g net carbs

Ingredients

- Vegetable broth 8 cups
- Olive oil 2 tbsp.
- Bell peppers, chopped, 2 large
- Garlic, minced 4 cloves
- Onion, chopped 1 large
- Cauliflower, 1-inch florets 1 medium head
- Diced tomatoes 2 cans (14.5-oz each)
- Green beans, cleaned 1-inch pieces 2 cups
- Italian seasoning 1 tbsp.
- Bay leaves dried 2 (optional)
- Black pepper, to taste (optional)
- Sea salt to taste, (optional)

Directions

1. In a pot, heat the olive oil on medium heat

2. Include the bell peppers and onions. Fry for 7 to 10 minutes till onions are just starting to brown.
3. Include the minced garlic and fry until fragrant for 1 minute.
4. Add the broth, green beans, cauliflower, Italian seasoning and diced tomatoes. Season with black pepper and sea salt to taste. Put in the bay leaves. Take it to a boil on high heat, decrease the heat to medium-low cover, and cook until vegetables are soft for about 12 to 18 minutes.

7. Red Curry Cauliflower Soup

Prep. Time: 15 minutes

Cook Time: 30 minutes

Servings: 8 servings

Serving size: 1cup

Nutrition as per serving

227kcal / 16 g fat / 18g carbs / 7g fiber / 6g protein = 11g net carbs

Ingredients

- Yellow onion, sliced 1 medium
- Garlic sliced 3 medium cloves
- Thai curry paste, red 4 oz. (about 4 tbsp.)
- Cauliflower florets 1 lb.
- Red lentils 1/2 cup
- Water 1 1/2 cups
- Vegetable broth, low-sodium 4 cups
- Himalayan pink salt 1/2 tsp.
- Black pepper 1/2 tsp.
- Coconut milk, unsweetened 1 can (14 oz.)
- Lemon juice 3 tbsp.
- Chives sliced 1 tbsp.

Directions

1. In a large saucepan, heat 3-4 tbsp. vegetable broth with the sliced onions until soft. Include the sliced garlic. Keep cooking for 1 to 2 minutes more until fragrant.
2. Add the cauliflower florets, red curry paste, water, red lentils, salt, black pepper, and 4 cups of vegetable broth into the saucepan. Heat the soup to a slow simmer and then decrease the heat to medium. Keep cooking until the red lentils and cauliflower are tender, stirring once in a while or for 15 to 20 minutes.
3. Pour the soup into a blender jug and completely blend the soup on high until it is smooth.
4. Transfer the blended soup to the saucepan and mix in the coconut milk on medium heat. Stir in the lemon juice and sprinkle chives on top before serving.

8. Thai Zucchini Noodles

Prep. Time: 15 minutes

Servings: 6 cups

Serving size: 1 cup

Nutrition as per serving

216kcal / 14g fat / 9g carbs / 4g fiber / 9g protein = 5g net carbs

Ingredients

- Grape tomatoes halved 1/2 cup
- Carrot julienned or spirals 1 large
- Red cabbage sliced thinly 1/2 cup
- Zucchini - thin or spiral noodles 1
- Thai basil 10 leaves
- For the peanut sauce:
- Garlic minced 1 clove
- Ginger fresh minced 1 tsp.
- Peanut butter creamy low carb 1 tbsp.
- Lime or lemon juice 1 tbsp.
- Soy sauce 1 tbsp.
- Red pepper flakes ¼ tsp.
- Cilantro leaves, peanuts unsalted roasted, and lime wedges for garnishing. (optional)

Directions

1. Whisk together the ginger, garlic, peanut butter, lime or lemon juice, red pepper flakes and soy sauce in a small bowl until well-blended and smooth. Add 1 to 2 tablespoon of water if it seems too thick, and blend.
2. Combine the carrots, zucchini noodles, red cabbage, basil leaves and tomatoes together. Mix in the peanut sauce. Lightly mix all together. Transfer all veggies and noodles to a serving platter.
3. Sprinkle a few peanuts and garnish wedges of lime if preferred. Enjoy!!

9. Creamy Tomato Soup

Prep. Time: 5 minutes

Cook Time: 5 minutes

Servings: 8 servings

Serving size: 1 cup

Nutrition as per serving

60kcal / 2g fat / 9g carbs / 2g fiber / 2g protein = 7g net carbs

Ingredients

- Vegetable broth 3 ½ cups
- Tomatoes with juice 3 cans (15oz)
- Green onions scallions 4
- Minced Garlic 1 tsp.
- Smoked paprika ½ tsp.
- Dried oregano 1 tsp.
- Basil 6 leaves
- Almond butter 2-3 tbsp.-optional
- Black pepper to taste
- Toasted almonds for topping -optional
- Salt to taste

Directions

1. Place all the ingredients in a large pot.
2. Heat to boiling, and decrease the heat to let it simmer till thick for about 20 min.
3. Blend the soup in a blender. Pour into bowls.
4. Sprinkle toasted nuts (if preferred) and serve.

Chapter 3- Dinner

1. Broccoli Fried Rice

Prep. Time: 5 minutes

Cook Time: 3 minutes

Servings: 4 servings

Serving size: 1 bowl

Nutrition as per serving

87kcal / 5g fat / 7g carbs / 4g fiber / 2g protein = 4.2g net carbs

Ingredients

- Broccoli, riced, (approx. 2 heads of broccoli) 4 cups
- Avocado oil 1 tbsp.
- Garlic finely chopped 1 tbsp.
- Coconut amino 1 tbsp.
- Toasted sesame oil 1 ½ tsp.
- Coarse salt ¼ to ½ tsp.
- Ginger grated ¼ - ½ tsp.
- Lime juice 1 tbsp. + more for serving
- Scallions, chopped 2 bulbs

- Parsley or cilantro, chopped 4 tbsp. (optional)
- Almonds sliced (optional)

Optional pairings:

- Shrimp, medium size, peeled & uncooked ½ lb.
- Fresh scallops 8-10
- Black pepper ⅛ tsp.
- Coarse salt ¼ tsp.

Directions

1. Heat a skillet to high, add olive oil. Add the finely chopped garlic with riced broccoli and sauté for 1 min. Season the rice with toasted sesame oil, coconut amino, and coarse salt. Fry for 2 min. more. The broccoli rice should be sautéed until it is just done and not mushy and maintains a bright green color.
2. Remove from heat and immediately add grated ginger to it. Also, add lime juice.
3. Sprinkle cilantro, sliced almonds and scallions. Arrange some lime wedges on the side and serve.

2. Low-carb vegan Grilled Tofu Skewers

Prep. Time: 15 minutes

Cook Time: 15 minutes

Servings: 6 servings

Serving size: 1 skewer

Nutrition as per serving

118kcal / 5.3g fat / 10g carbs / 1.8g fiber / 10.6g protein = 8g net carbs

Ingredients

- Tofu 1 block (180 g)
- Yellow bell pepper 1
- Zucchini 2 small
- Cherry tomatoes 2 cups
- Red bell pepper 1
- Red onion 1
- Soy sauce 2 tbsp.
- Barbecue sauce 3 tsp.
- Sesame seeds 2 tsp.
- Pepper
- Salt

Directions

1. Press the tofu to remove its liquid for at least half an hour. Afterward, cut it into cubes and soak in soy sauce
2. Cut the veggies: cut bell peppers, slice zucchini, and chop red onions into small squares. Every piece should be cut to the same size.
3. Prepare skewers: stick the veggies and tofu one after the other on bamboo sticks till all the vegetables have been used up.
4. Heat a grill pan or a frying pan till sizzling hot, brush some olive oil on it and assemble skewers in it, cooking for a few minutes on every side, till the veggies turn soft, not soggy, and the peppers begin getting a char. The tofu will turn golden brown. Sprinkle some pepper and salt when all is cooked, brush some barbecue sauce on the skewers, sprinkle on little sesame seeds. Take off from grill or pan.
5. Serve hot.

3. Zucchini Alfredo Pasta

Prep. Time: 15 minutes

Cook Time: 15 minutes

Servings: 2 Servings

Serving size: ½ of the recipe

Nutrition as per serving

225kcal / 16g fat / 19g carbs / 6g fiber / 14g protein = 12g net carbs

- **Ingredients**
- Zucchinis spiralized 2 medium
- Vegan Parmesan 1-2 Tbsp. (optional)
- Quick Alfredo Sauce
- Raw cashews soaked 1/2 cup
- Lemon juice 2 Tbsp.
- Garlic powder 1/2 tsp.
- Nutritional yeast 3 Tbsp.
- White miso (can sub soy sauce, coconut amino or tamari,) 2 tsp.
- Onion powder 1 tsp.
- Water ¼ - ½ cup

Directions

1. Spiralize the zucchini to make noodles. In a large saucepan, heat a little olive oil and add the zucchini noodles. Sauté for a few minutes and remove from heat.
2. Put all ingredients for the Alfredo into a blender (begin with ¼ cup water), then blend until creamy. If the sauce seems too thick, add a few tablespoons of water until the desired consistency is reached.
3. Top the zucchini noodles with hot Alfredo sauce and sprinkle a little vegan parmesan if desired.

4. Low-Carb Shiitake Mushroom Fried Rice

Prep. Time: 5 minutes

Cook Time: 25 minutes

Servings: 8 servings

Serving size: 1 cup

Nutrition as per serving

90kcal / 3g fat / 12g carbs / 5g fiber / 7g protein = 7g net carbs

Ingredients

- Frozen vegetables (peas, edamame, and carrots,) 10 oz.
- Frozen cauliflower rice 4 cups
- Frozen shiitake mushrooms 10 oz.
- Onion diced 1 medium
- Fresh ginger grated 2-inch
- Garlic minced 3 cloves
- Water 3-4 tbsp.
- Tamari, low-sodium 3 tbsp.
- Green onions, sliced thinly 1/2 cup
- Toasted sesame oil 1/2 tsp.

Directions

1. Over medium heat, fry the chopped onions with 3 to 4 tbsp. of water in a big pan until the onions are translucent and soft. Include the minced garlic and grated ginger. Combine all together and keep cooking until fragrant or for 2-3 minutes.
2. Add the cauliflower rice, mushrooms, and frozen mixed vegetables to the pan. Mix to combine, raising the flame to medium-high. Keep cooking for approx. 15 minutes or till all the veggies are tender and hot and also the water has evaporated.
3. A small bowl mix together toasted sesame oil and low-sodium tamari and pour on the veggies and mix it in. sprinkle sliced green onions and serve.

5. Portobello Pizza Keto Stuffed Mushrooms Recipe

Prep. Time: 10 minutes

Cook Time: 20 minutes

Servings: 4 servings

Serving size: 1 stuffed mushroom

Nutrition as per serving

113kcal / 6g fat / 5g carbs / 1g fiber / 7g protein = 4g net carbs

Ingredients

- Olive oil spray
- Portobello mushrooms, remove stems 4 large
- Marinara sauce, low-carb 1/2 cup
- Mozzarella cheese shredded 1/2 cup
- Pepperoni sausage (or a chorizo link, sliced thinly) 16 slices

Directions

1. Heat the oven up to 190 degrees C. Line parchment paper on a baking tray spraying it with olive oil spray.
2. Scoop out the dark gills of the mushrooms using a spoon, and throw away the gills.
3. Assemble the mushrooms with the stem side up, and on it, add 2 tbsp. of sauce on each. Add 2 tbsp. of mozzarella and four slices of pepperoni on each.
4. Put it in the oven for 20 to 25 minutes, till the cheese is melted and bubbly and the mushrooms are done. Serve hot.

6. Easy Broccoli Soup

Prep. Time: 10 minutes

Cook Time: 25 minutes

Servings: 6 servings

Serving size: 1 cup

Nutrition as per serving

171 kcal/ 13g fat / 8g carbs / 2g fiber / 3g protein = 6g net carbs

Ingredients

- Cauliflower florets 1 cup
- Broccoli 1 pound
- Vegan cheese cheddar style 1-2 tbsp. - optional
- Coconut milk full fat 1 cup
- Water 1 cup
- Onion 1 medium
- Bay leaves 2 small
- Garlic 2 cloves
- Olive oil 2 tbsp.
- Salt
- Nutritional yeasts 3 tbsp.
- Black pepper powder 1 tsp.

Directions

1. Over medium heat, add olive oil to a pan.
2. Add garlic and bay leaves and fry till the garlic is golden.
3. Add in the chopped onions and fry till they are translucent.
4. Add the cauliflower florets and fry for 2 minutes.
5. Put in the broccoli florets and fry for 8 minutes or till the raw odor is gone.
6. Take off heat. Leave it to cool, and then blend into a paste, adding a cup of water.
7. Put on the stove again, add the coconut milk and boil the mixture.
8. Then add the salt, black pepper, nutritional yeast, and keep on stirring.
9. Simmer for about 6-8 minutes. Serve hot!

7. Vegan Thai Soup

Prep. Time: 10 minutes

Cook Time: 15 minutes

Servings: 3-4 servings

Serving size: 1/4 of the recipe

Nutrition as per serving

339 kcal / 27.6g fat / 15.2g carbs / 3.2g fiber / 14.8g protein = 12g net carbs

Ingredients

- Mushrooms sliced 3
- Red onion, julienned 1/2
- Ginger root, peeled and chopped finely 1/2-inch piece
- Red bell pepper julienned 1/2
- Garlic, chopped finely 2 cloves
- Thai chili, chopped finely 1/2
- Water or preferably vegetable broth 2 cups
- Coconut sugar or any Keto substitute 1 tbsp.
- Coconut milk 1 can (14-oz.)
- Firm tofu, cut in squares 10 oz.
- Soy sauce or tamari 1 tbsp.
- Fresh cilantro, chopped a handful
- Lime juice 2 tsp.

Directions

1. In a big pot, add all the veggies (mushrooms, onion, garlic, ginger, red bell pepper, and Thai chili), coconut milk broth, and sugar.
2. Take it to a rolling boil and then let cook for 5 minutes over medium heat.
3. Then add the cubed tofu and cook for another 5 minutes.
4. Take off the heat, then add the lime juice, tamari, and fresh cilantro. Mix and serve.
5. Store the soup in an airtight container in the refrigerator for up to 6 days. It can also be frozen.

8. Cauliflower Fried Rice

Prep. Time: 5 minutes

Cook Time: 10 minutes

Servings: 2 servings

Serving size: 3 cups

Nutrition as per serving

289kcal / 14g fat / 30.2g carbs / 15g fiber / 12g protein = 15g net carbs

Ingredients

- Cauliflower, riced 1 small
- Garlic, minced 5 cloves
- Sesame oil 2 tbsp.
- Mixed vegetables (onions, peas, bell pepper, carrots,) 1 ½ cup
- Pepper to taste
- Salt, to taste

Optional add-ons:

- Thai peanut sauce
- Tamari 2 tbsp.
- Curry powder 2 tsp.
- Scallions, chopped 5
- Sesame seeds 4 tsp.

Directions

1. Wash and cut the cauliflower into florets. Put the florets into a food processor and process till it becomes rice-like.
2. In a large pot or pan, heat the sesame oil, and add minced garlic, carrots, onions, bell pepper, peas, and scallions if using. Sauté all for about 3 minutes.

3. Then add the cauliflower rice and sauté for another 5 minutes, add pepper and salt. Add the optional add-ons; Thai peanut sauce and curry powder, mix for 2 minutes. Take out in bowls or plates sprinkle with the sesame seeds if you like.

9. Indian Baingan Bharta

Prep. Time: 15 minutes

Cook Time: 15 minutes

Servings: 4 servings

Serving size: ¼ of the recipe

Nutrition as per serving

222kcal /14g fat / 23g carbs / 8g fiber / 4g protein = 15g net carbs

Ingredients

- Eggplants 2 medium
- Onion, sliced 1 medium
- Olive oil ¼ cup
- Garlic, diced 4 cloves
- Tomato chopped 1 medium
- Cumin seeds ½ tsp.
- Turmeric powder ½ tsp.
- Chili powder ½ tsp.
- Salt, to taste
- Green chili, chopped 1
- Fresh cilantro, chopped 1 sprig

Directions

1. On an open flame, roast both the eggplants. When one side is done, turn to cook the other side. The eggplant will shrink and sag, and the skins will become wrinkled when it is cooked from inside. Leave to cool, and then peel the skin as much as possible and mash.
2. In a frying pan or skillet, heat oil and sauté the onions till reddish brown. Add garlic and cumin.
3. Stir and add the tomatoes, chili powders, turmeric and salt. Fry on medium heat until the tomatoes become soft and all is cooked thoroughly.
4. Add the mashed eggplant to the tomato mixture and cook for a couple of minutes.
5. Sprinkle fresh cilantro and chopped green chili on top and serve.

Chapter 4- Salads

1. Vegan Arugula Avocado Tomato Salad

Prep. Time: 20 minutes

Servings: 8 servings

Serving size: 1cup

Nutrition as per serving

134kcal / 9g fat / 12g carbs / 10g fiber / 3g protein = 2g net carbs

Ingredients

For Balsamic Vinaigrette

- Lemon juice 1 tbsp.
- Balsamic vinegar 2 tbsp.
- Olive oil 1 tbsp.
- Maple syrup 1 tbsp.
- Black pepper 1/4 tsp.
- Garlic minced 1 small clove
- Himalayan pink salt 1/4 tsp.

For Arugula Salad

- Baby arugula chopped roughly 5 oz.
- Basil leaves sliced thinly 6 large
- Red and yellow grape tomatoes halve 1 pint each
- Avocados chopped 2 large

- Red onion minced 1/2 cup

Directions

1. In a large salad bowl, add the sliced basil leaves and roughly chopped arugula. Include the minced red onion, avocado chunks, and sliced grape tomatoes into the bowl. Mix to combine.
2. In a measuring cup, whisk together olive oil, balsamic vinegar, lemon juice, maple syrup, garlic clove, black pepper and salt, until combined well.
3. Drizzle all the balsamic dressing on the salad. Lightly mix the salad till all is coated in the dressing. Serve the salad on a large platter.

2. Triple Green Kale Salad

Prep. Time: 14 minutes

Cook Time: 1 minute

Servings: 4 servings

Serving size: ¼ of the recipe

Nutrition as per serving

135kcal / 10g fat / 10g carbs / 3g fiber / 3g protein = 7g net carbs

Ingredients

Green 1

- Lacinato kale, torn to small piece 8-10 oz.
- Toasted sesame oil 2 tsp.
- Flaxseed oil or olive oil extra virgin, 2 tsp.
- Garlic cloves, crushed or grated 2 small
- Fresh ginger grated 1 tsp.
- Coarse sea salt a pinch

Green 2

- Snow peas, cut into pieces, a large handful
- Coconut amino 2 tsp.
- Ripe avocado, sliced 1
- Balsamic vinegar 2 tsp.
- Scallions, cut into small pieces, a small handful
- Hemp seeds
- Orange zest

Directions

1. Wash and dry the kale thoroughly. On a cutting board, put the kale leaf and remove each leaf's center stems with a paring knife. Remove the stems from all the leaves. Pile 4-5 kale leaves and slice them into smaller pieces.

2. Mix the chopped kale leaves and all the ingredients of "green 1". Lightly massage the kale with clean hands, rubbing the oil with the leaves.
3. Add the ingredients of "green 2". Toss and serve chilled

3. Tomato Cucumber Salad

Prep. Time: 10 minutes

Servings: 4 servings

Serving size: 2 large portions or 4 small sides

Nutrition as per serving

176 kcal / 14g fat / 13g carbs / 5g fiber / 2g protein = 8g net carbs

Ingredients

- Green bell pepper 1
- Cherry tomatoes (quartered) 1 ½ cups
- Ripe avocados 1-2
- English cucumber 1
- Avocado oil 1/8 - 1/4 cup
- Red wine vinegar 1 tbsp.
- Lemon, juiced 1
- Fresh cilantro 2 tbsp.
- Pepper to taste
- Salt to taste

Directions

1. Cut the veggies, discarding any skin, seeds, and stems not needed.
2. Blend together oil, lemon juice, vinegar, pepper, salt, and fresh herbs that you like and drizzle all over the salad.
3. Mix together to coat well and serve!

4. Best Homemade Vegan Ranch

Prep. Time: 10 minutes

Servings: 8 servings

Serving size: 1½ tablespoon

Nutrition as per serving

138kcal / 11g fat / 8g carbs / 1g fiber / 5g protein = 7g net carbs

Ingredients

- Raw cashew pieces 1 1/2 cups
- Water 3/4 cup
- Rice vinegar 2 tbsp.
- Lemon juice 2 tbsp.
- Salt 1 tsp.
- Garlic powder 1 1/2 tsp.
- Onion powder 1 1/2 tsp.
- Fresh dill 1/4 cup of dried dill 2-3 tsp.

Directions

1. In hot water, soak the raw cashews for more than 5-10 minutes.
2. Strain the cashews and put them into a blender. Add all ingredients, excluding the dill, and process until very smooth.
3. Now include the dill, and give it a pulse or two to combine. Don't blend the dill; otherwise, it will be very green.
4. Drizzle on salads or as a dip with fresh veggies. Will keep in the fridge for up to 6 days. If it thickens in the fridge, add water to thin it out to the desired consistency

5. Vegan Sesame Ginger Coleslaw

Prep. Time: 30 minutes

Servings: 12 servings

Serving size: 1 cup

Nutrition as per serving

66kcal / 2g fat / 11g carbs / 3g fiber / 3g protein = 8g net carbs

Ingredients

For sesame ginger dressing -

- Almond butter 2 tbsp.
- Tahini 1 tbsp.
- Tamari, low-sodium 2 tbsp.

- Rice vinegar 2 tbsp.
- Fresh ginger peeled 2-inch knob
- Lime juice 3 tbsp.
- Hot sauce 1 tbsp.
- Garlic peeled 1 medium clove
- Maple syrup 1 tbsp.

For coleslaw -

- Red cabbage sliced thinly 5 cups
- Carrots sliced thinly 2 cups
- Green cabbage sliced thinly 5 cups
- Green onions sliced 1 cup
- Cilantro chopped roughly 1 cup

Directions

1. In a blender, add tahini. Almond butter, tamari, lime juice, rice vinegar, maple syrup, hot sauce, ginger and garlic clove, and blend on high speed until creamy and smooth.
2. In a large bowl, thinly sliced carrots, green and red cabbage, cilantro, and green onions. Drizzle the dressing all over the veggie mixture, and then toss to combine.
3. Refrigerate covered for 1 hour. Serve chilled

Notes

Before you add the dressing, salting the cabbage helps to draw out the extra liquid. This way, the slaw will not get soggy when stored for a few days in the fridge.

Chapter 5- Snacks

1. Vegan Lemon Curd

Prep. Time: 5 minutes

Cook Time: 10 minutes

Servings: 9 servings

Serving size: 1.75tbsp

Nutrition as per serving

5kcal / 0g fat / 0g carbs / 0g fiber / 0g protein = 0g net carbs

Ingredients

- Lemon 1 large
- Almond milk or coconut milk 1 cup
- Lemon stevia or monk fruit drops ¼ tsp.
- Xanthum gum 1 tsp.
- Turmeric powder a pinch optional

Directions

1. In a blender, blend together almond milk, lemon juice and zest from a large lemon and stevia lemon/monk fruit drops
2. Transfer the mixture to a medium saucepan. Slowly stir in xanthum gum. Boil the mixture and remove it from heat.
3. Transfer to a container. Leave it to cool before covering. It will thicken as it gets cold. Keep in the refrigerator for up to a week.

2. Crispy Cauliflower Wings

Prep. Time: 5 minutes

Cook Time: 40 minutes

Servings: 6 servings

Serving size: 1 cup

Nutrition as per serving

48kcal / 4.3g fat / 1g carbs / 1g fiber / 2g protein = 0g net carbs

Ingredients

- Hot sauce 3-4 tbsp.
- Almond flour 1 tbsp.
- Avocado oil 1 tbsp.
- Salt to taste
- Cauliflower head (cut into bites, washed and pat dried) 1

Directions

1. Heat oven up to 180c / 160c / 350f / gas 6.
2. Combine avocado oil, almond flour, hot sauce and salt together in a large mixing bowl.
3. Mix in the cauliflower and coat well.
4. In a single layer, assemble the cauliflower on a foil-lined baking sheet.
5. Bake for 35-40 min. Halfway through, take out the baking sheet, mix the cauliflower, and bake until its edges are crispy and done. Take out and put aside.
6. Serve warm or cold according to your preference, with some hot sauce dip

3. Vegan Seed Cheese

Prep. Time: 10 minutes

Servings: 6

Serving size: 1 tablespoon

Nutrition as per serving

150kcal / 11g fat / 3g carbs / 3g fiber / 7g protein = 0g net carbs

Ingredients

- Seeds sunflower, pumpkin, or a blend 1 cup
- Water 1/2 cup
- Apple cider vinegar 2 tbsp.
- Nutritional yeast 2 tbsp.
- Salt ¼ tsp. suppose using salted seeds/ if using unsalted seeds ¾ tsp.
- Seasonings to taste

Directions

1. Combine all ingredients in a food processor and process.
2. Leave for ten minutes.
3. Process again until creamy and smooth.
4. Enjoy!

4. Easy & Authentic Guacamole

Prep. Time: 10 minutes

Servings: 4 servings

Serving size: ½ cup

Nutrition as per serving

184.8kcal / 15.3g fat / 12.3g carbs / 7.6g fiber / 2.5g protein = 5g net carbs

Ingredients

- Avocados, ripe 3
- Onion, diced finely 1/2 small
- Roma tomatoes, diced 2
- Fresh cilantro finely chopped 3 tbsp.
- Jalapeno pepper, finely diced and seeds removed 1
- Garlic, minced2 cloves
- Lime juice 1
- Sea salt 1/2 tsp.

Directions

1. Cut the avocados into halves, removing the pit; scoop the avocado pulp into a large mixing bowl.
2. With a fork, mash the avocado pulp making it as smooth or chunky as you would like.
3. Add all the other ingredients and mix. Taste and modify seasoning by adding more lime juice or a pinch of salt if needed.
4. Pour the guacamole into a serving bowl and serve with low-carb Keto crackers (recipe below).

5. Almond Flour Low-Carb Keto Crackers

Prep. Time: 10 minutes

Cook Time: 15 minutes

Servings: 6 Servings

Serving size: ½ cup

Nutrition as per serving

151kcal / 13g fat / 6g carbs / 3g fiber / 4g protein = 3g net carbs

Ingredients

- Almond flour 1 cup
- Sunflower seeds 2 tbsp.
- Flax meal or whole psyllium husks 1 tablespoon
- Sea salt ¾ tsp. Or to taste
- Water 2 tbsp.
- Olive oil or coconut oil one tablespoon

Directions

1. Heat oven up to 350°f.
2. In a food processor, blend together sunflower seeds, almond flour, sea salt and psyllium, until the sunflower seeds are finely chopped.
3. Add in the coconut and oil-water and pulse until a dough forms
4. Place a parchment paper on a flat surface and place and press the dough ball flat on it. Top with another parchment sheet and roll the dough to a thickness of ⅛ - 1/16 of an inch.
5. Remove the top parchment sheet, and with a knife or pizza cutter, cut into one-inch squares. If desired, sprinkle with sea salt.
6. Transfer the cut dough onto a baking tray and bake in a preheated oven at 350°f until edges are crisp and brown (around 10-15 minutes). Leave on a rack to cool and breaks into squares.

6. Oven-Baked Healthy Zucchini Chips

Prep. Time: 10 minutes

Cook Time: 2 hours

Servings: 8 servings

Serving size: 12 zucchini chips

Nutrition as per serving

23kcal / 2g fat / 2g carbs / 1g fiber / 1g protein = 1g net carbs

Ingredients

- Zucchini 2 medium
- Avocado oil (or olive oil) 1 tbsp.
- Sea salt 1/2 tsp

Directions

1. Heat the oven up to 93 degrees C (200 degrees F).
2. Slice the zucchini into .3 cm (1/8 in) thin slices.

3. Toss the zucchini slices in olive oil and coat them thoroughly. Lightly sprinkle with salt. Mix to coat again.
4. Place a cooling rack covered with parchment paper on two cookie trays. (This method permits better circulation of air.) In a single layer, assemble the zucchini slices on it. Do not overlap.
5. Put in the oven for about two and a half hours, turning the pans 90 degrees halfway through. When the zucchini chips begin to get golden and crispy, they are. Turn off the oven and leave them there to cool with the door open slightly (as they cool, they will become crisper).

7. 8-Ingredient Zucchini Lasagna

Prep. Time: 20 minutes

Cook Time: 1 hour

Servings: 9 squares

Serving size: 1 square

Nutrition as per serving

395kcal / 35.3g fat / 19g carbs / 10g fiber / 6.8g protein = 9g net carbs

Ingredients

- Organic tomato basil marinara sauce 1 jars (28-oz.)
- Zucchini squash, sliced thinly 3 medium (or substitute with eggplant)

For vegan ricotta

- Soaked blanched almonds or raw macadamia nuts 3 cups (or extra firm tofu, strained and dry pressed for 10 minutes 1 block of 16-oz.)
- Nutritional yeast 2 tbsp.
- Fresh basil chopped finely 1/2 cup
- Dried oregano 2 tsp.
- Lemon, medium 2 Tbsp.
- Olive oil, extra virgin 1 tbsp. (optional)
- Sea salt 1 tsp.
- Black pepper a pinch
- Water 1/2 cup
- Vegan parmesan cheese 1/4 cup + more for topping (optional)

Directions

1. Heat oven up to 375 degrees F
2. Add almond or macadamia nuts or crumbled tofu to a blender or food processor and combine and scrape down the sides when needed. It should become a fine meal.
3. Then include the remaining ingredients: fresh basil, Nutritional yeast, oregano, olive oil (if using), lemon juice, pepper, salt, vegan parmesan cheese (if using) and water. It should become a well-puréed paste or mixture.

4. Check the seasonings, and add more pepper and salt for flavor, lemon juice for vividness and nutritional yeast for cheesier flavor, as needed.
5. Pour about a cup of marinara sauce into a baking dish of 9×13-inch and assemble the thinly sliced zucchini in overlapping lines.
6. Place small scoops of the vegan ricotta mixture all over the layered zucchini and spread it gently into a thin layer. Apply a layer of the marinara sauce and then layer more zucchini slices. Carry on till all zucchini and filling are used up. The zucchini and sauce should be the last two layers. Scatter some vegan parmesan cheese (if using) on top, covering with the foil.
7. Place in oven covered to bake for 45 minutes, then take off the foil and bake for another 15 minutes. When done, the zucchini should tender enough to be easily pierced with a knife. Leave to rest for 10 to 15 minutes.
8. Serve hot with fresh basil and more vegan parmesan cheese on top. Keep Leftovers in the refrigerator for 2-3 days, or freeze for up to 1 month.

8. Sunflower Courgetti Seed Cheese

Prep. Time: 20 minutes

Servings: 6 servings

Serving size: 2 tablespoon

Nutrition as per serving

286cals / 22g fat / 17gcarbs / 8g fiber / 13g protein = 4g net carbs

Ingredients

- Sunflower seeds 1 cup
- Zucchini /courgette 3
- Nutritional yeast 3 tbsp.
- Garlic 1 clove
- Sesame seeds 3 tbsp.
- Turmeric ¼ tsp.
- Apple cider vinegar 1 tbsp.
- Salt 2 pinches
- Water for blending and soaking
- Cherry tomatoes 6
- Fresh basil leaves 12

Directions

1. Immerse the sunflower seeds in water with a pinch of salt overnight or for at least an hour.
2. Strain the sunflower seeds and place them in a blender with garlic, nutritional yeast, turmeric, sesame, and vinegar.
3. Just add enough water into the blender so that it turns into a smooth paste.
4. A spiralizer makes the zucchini /courgette into noodles or makes them into thin strips with a vegetable peeler.

5. Add a pinch of salt to the spiralized noodles and massage them until it reduces in volume and releases its juices.
6. Mix in the cheese mixture and enjoy.

9. Vegan Garlic Aioli

Prep. Time: 5 minutes

Servings: 8 servings

Serving size: 1 tablespoon

Nutrition as per serving

138kcal / 14g fat / 2g carbs / 1g fiber / 1g protein = 1g net carbs

Ingredients

- Original vegenaise 3/4 cup
- Fresh lemon juice 2 ½ tbsp.
- Garlic minced 3 medium cloves
- Himalayan pink salt ¼ tsp.
- Black pepper¼ tsp

Directions

In a small bowl, add all the ingredients and combine with a whisk. Refrigerate covered for 30 minutes. Serve chilled.

Notes

Store the remaining aioli in a sealed container in the refrigerator for 5 to 7 days.

Vegan garlic aioli cannot be frozen as vegan mayo splits, and the consistency doesn't remain the same.

Chapter 6- Side Dishes

1. Asian Cucumber Salad

Prep. Time: 10 minutes

Wait Time: 15 minutes

Servings: 2

Serving size: 1.5 cups

Nutrition as per serving

70 cal. / 14.3g fat / 6g carbs / 3g fiber / 3g protein = 3g net carbs

Ingredients

- Scallions, thinly sliced 2
- English cucumber 1
- Table salt 1/4 tsp.
- For the dressing:
- Soy sauce 2 tsp.
- Toasted sesame oil 2 tsp.
- Rice vinegar or white vinegar 1 tsp.
- Sesame seeds, white or black 1/2 tsp.
- Red pepper flakes crushed 1/2 tsp.

Directions

1. Prepping the cucumber: slice 1/2-inch thick rounds of the cucumber, then chop each coin into 3 to 5 small wedges. In a medium bowl, sprinkle salt on the wedges and toss. Leave it at room temperature until they release liquid, about 15 to 30 minutes. Discard the liquid and pat dry the cucumber wedges with a paper towel to absorb moisture until the wedges are almost dry to touch.
2. Mix the salad: To a bowl, add the dried cucumbers, scallions and all ingredients for the dressing. Stir until combined. After tasting, add more dressing ingredients if required.
3. Serving: serve immediately after preparation; otherwise, the cucumbers will release more water and lose their crunch. Serve it as a side dish or refreshing appetizer with heavy meat-centric meals like chicken adobo, beef stir fry, or pork stir fry.

2. Oven Roasted Lemon Garlic Asparagus

Prep. Time: 10 minutes

Cook Time: 12 minutes

Servings: 4

Serving size: ¼ of the recipe

Nutrition as per serving

67kcal / 4g fat / 5 g carbs / 2g fiber / 2g protein = 3g net carbs

Ingredients

- Asparagus (1/2 inch thick stalks about 25-30) 1 lb.
- Olive oil 1 tbsp.
- Dried thyme 1/4 tsp.
- Vegan parmesan cheese 1-2 tbsp.
- Onion granules 1/4 tsp.
- Garlic, minced 2 cloves
- Lemon zest 1 tsp.
- Himalayan sea salt to taste
- Pepper to taste
- Fresh lemon juice 1 tbsp.
- Lemon 4-5 slices
- Olive oil 1 tsp.

Directions

1. Heat the oven up to 425 degrees.
2. Prepare the Asparagus: Wash and dry the asparagus thoroughly. Cut the base of each stalk of 1 to 1 ½ inch off the bottom.
3. Line a tray with parchment and place the asparagus spears on it. Drizzle a tablespoon of olive oil all over the asparagus spears and mix to coat each piece. Add onion granules,

thyme, lemon zest, pepper and sea salt all over the oiled asparagus and mix one more time. Place lemon slices on top and bake for about 8 minutes.

4. In a small bowl, add the crushed garlic cloves and a tablespoon of olive oil and mix both together. When the asparagus has baked for 8 minutes, remove the tray, add the minced garlic evenly all over the asparagus. Place it back in the oven and again bake for 3 to 4 more minutes.

5. Take out the tray when the asparagus is tender; it must still be bright green and not mushy. Squeeze about a tablespoon of lemon over the asparagus and sprinkle with shredded vegan parmesan cheese.

3. Zucchini Noodles with Avocado Sauce

Prep. Time: 10 minutes

Servings: 2

Serving size: 1/2 of the recipe

Nutrition as per serving

313kcal / 26.8g fat / 18.7g carbs / 9.7g fiber / 6.8g protein = 9 g net carbs

Ingredients

- Zucchini 1
- Cherry tomatoes sliced 12
- Basil 1 1/4 cup
- Avocado 1
- Pine nuts 4 tbsp.
- Water 1/3 cup
- Lemon juice 2 tbsp.

Directions

1. Using a spiralizer or a peeler, cut the zucchini noodles.
2. Apart from the cherry tomatoes, put all the ingredients in a blender and blend until smooth to make avocado sauce.
3. Combine avocado sauce, zucchini noodles, and cherry tomatoes in a large mixing bowl.
4. It's recommended to serve these avocado sauce zucchini noodles fresh, but they can also be stored in the fridge for about 1 to 2 days.

4. Zucchini Tomato Pesto Veggie Bake

Prep. Time: 25 minutes

Cook Time: 35 minutes

Servings: 6

Serving size: 1/6 of the recipe

Nutrition as per serving

127kcal / 9g fat / 11g carbs / 3g fiber / 3g protein = 8g net carbs

Ingredients

Pesto sauce

- Fresh basil leaves 2 cups
- Garlic peeled 1 clove
- Pine nuts 1/4 cup (or raw pumpkin seeds)
- Olive oil 3 tbsp.
- Lemon juice 2 tbsp.
- Black pepper 1/8 tsp.
- Himalayan pink salt 1/4 tsp.

Vegetables

- Zucchini sliced thinly 3 medium
- Red onions sliced thinly 4 small
- Roma tomatoes sliced thinly 8 medium
- Olive oil 1 tbsp.

Directions

1. Prepare the pesto sauce. Add the fresh pumpkin seeds, basil leaves, garlic, olive oil, lemon juice, water pepper, salt, and a food processor or blender. Blend the sauce till smooth and put it aside for the future.
2. Heat the oven to 350 degrees. Slice thinly the red onions, zucchini, and tomatoes, about 1/8"- 1/4" thick. Make sure the veggies are cut in uniform size to bake evenly.

3. Lightly oil a cast-iron skillet with a brush. Assemble the sliced veggies in the skillet in the following order: zucchini, red onion, zucchini, and tomato. Keep on the process till all the veggies are done with. Begin in the outer edge first, going in circles towards the center.
4. Pour the vegan pesto sauce evenly all over the veggies, and then with a silicone brush, spread the sauce all over the veggies in the pan.
5. Top a sheet of unbleached parchment paper on the veggies and put in the oven for 30-35 minutes or till all the veggies are tender.

5. Tomato Mushroom Spaghetti Squash

Prep. Time: 30 minutes

Cook Time: 10 minutes

Servings: 6

Serving size: 1 bowl

Nutrition as per serving

173 kcal/ 12g fat / 17g carbs / 4g fiber / 4g protein = 12g net carbs

Ingredients

- Spaghetti squash, 1 large, about 6 cups.
- Tomatoes diced 2 cups
- Garlic minced 4 cloves
- Mushrooms sliced 8 oz.
- Onions or shallots, chopped, 1/3 cup about 1 small
- Pine nuts toasted 1/4 cup
- Fresh basil, a handful,
- Olive oil 3 tbsp.
- Black pepper to taste
- Kosher salt to taste
- red pepper flakes pinch

Directions

1. Cook the spaghetti squash. Once sufficiently cool, slice in half, discard seeds and stringy pieces and strip with 2 forks. Put it aside.
2. Heat oil in a large frypan over medium heat. Fry mushrooms and onions, stirring continuously, for about 3 to 4 minutes. Add in garlic and stir until fragrant, 1 to 2 minutes. Don't overcook the garlic.
3. Include tomatoes and keep stirring.
4. Include the cooked spaghetti squash, then toss till squash is heated through and veggies are evenly distributed.
5. Stir in toasted pine nuts and fresh basil. Season with pepper, a pinch of red pepper flakes and kosher salt to taste

6. Roasted Cabbage with Lemon

Prep. Time: 5 minutes

Cook Time: 30 minutes

Servings: 4

Serving size: 1

Nutrition as per serving

78 kcal / 7g fat / 5g carbs / 1g fiber / 1g protein = 4g net carbs

Ingredients

- Green cabbage 1 large head
- Olive oil 2 tbsp.
- Freshly squeezed lemon juice 3 tbsp.
- sea salt a generous amount
- black pepper freshly ground a generous amount
- lemon slices, (optional)

Directions

1. Heat the oven up to 450f. Apply non-stick spray on a roasting pan.
2. Cutting through the stem end and core, slice the cabbage's head into eight same-size wedges. Place wedges in the roasting pan in a single layer.
3. Mix the lemon juice and olive oil. With a pastry brush, apply the mixture on each cabbage wedge, then generously season with fresh ground black pepper salt. Flip over the cabbage wedges carefully, and brush and season this side too.
4. Bake the cabbage until the wedges' undersides are nicely browned, for about 15 minutes. Removing the pan from the oven, flip each wedge carefully.
5. Place in the oven again and roast for 10 to 15 minutes more, till the wedges are cooked thoroughly, nicely brown and with a bit of chewiness remaining.
6. Serve immediately, with extra lemon slices.

7. Keto Roasted Radishes

Prep. Time: 5 minutes

Cook Time: 30 minutes

Servings: 6

Serving size: 1 cup

Nutrition as per serving

25kcal / 1g fat / 1g carbs / 1g fiber / 1g protein = 0g net carbs

Ingredients

- Radishes 20-25 (similar size)
- Vegetable broth 1/2 cup
- Garlic minced 3 cloves
- Dried rosemary 1/2 tsp.
- Fresh rosemary 1 sprig (optional)
- Dried oregano 1/4 tsp.
- Onion Powder 1/2 tsp.
- Black pepper 1/4 tsp.
- Salt 1/4 tsp.

Directions

1. Heat the oven up to 400 degrees.
2. Prep the radishes by rinsing them well and cutting off the roots greens, and stems. Chop each radish in half. Make into quarters if they are bigger to cook quickly.
3. In a medium-sized casserole, add the minced garlic, vegetable broth, onion powder, rosemary, oregano, black pepper and salt. Stirring well to mix the seasonings.
4. Transfer all the radishes into the casserole, toss with the broth to coat all radishes and then bake, covered for about 30-35 minutes (if the radishes are on the small side, check them at 25 minutes) or till the radishes are tender, stirring in between.
5. Sprinkle fresh rosemary just before serving (optional). Keep leftovers in a sealed container in the refrigerator for 4-5 days.

Chapter 7- Desserts

1. Easy Vegan Fat Bombs

Prep. Time: 10 minutes

Freeze Time: 1-2 hours

Servings: 12 fat bombs

Serving size: 3 fat bombs

Nutrition as per serving

320 kcal / 35g fat / 5g carbs / 3g fiber / 3g protein = 2g net carbs

Ingredients

- Stevia 6 drops
- Macadamia nut butter warmed ¾ cup
- Coconut oil, melted or room temperature ¼ cup

Directions

1. In the microwave or a saucepan, heat macadamia nut butter until warm.
2. Pour in coconut oil and stevia drops. Mix.
3. Spoon mixture into mini muffin tins or silicone molds and chill for about 1-2 hours.
4. When set, take out of molds and enjoy!
5. Keep in a sealed box in the freezer.

2. Coconut Fat Bombs

Prep. Time: 10 minutes

Freeze Time: 1 hour

Servings: 18

Serving size: 1 fat bomb

Nutrition as per serving

86kcal / 9g fat / 1g carbs / 0g fiber / 0g protein = 1g net carbs

Ingredients

- Coconut Butter melted ½ cup
- Coconut finely shredded 2 tbsp. + ¼ cup
- Coconut oil, melted ½ cup
- Stevia 12 drops

Directions

1. Combine all ingredients; fill an ice cube tray or mini muffin liners with a tablespoon putting one spoonful in each. Chill for 1 hour. Keep in the fridge.

3. Peanut butter coconut truffles

Prep. Time: 20 minutes

Freeze Time: 1 hour 10 minutes

Servings: 22 truffles

Serving size: 2 truffles

Nutrition as per serving

126kcal / 11g fat / 4g carbs / 1g fiber / 3g protein = 3g net carbs

Ingredients

- Creamy peanut butter ½ cup
- Coconut oil 1 tbsp.
- Toasted coconut butter, melted ½ cup
- Shredded coconut, ½ cup + more to garnish
- Chopped peanuts, ½ cup + more to garnish
- Sea salt, ¼ tsp. optional
- Sugar-free chocolate ⅔ cup
- Stevia 10 drops

Directions

2. In a large mixing bowl, mix together the melted coconut butter, peanut butter, chopped peanuts, coconut, stevia drops and salt. Tasting to adjust amounts of salt and stevia if desired.

3. Chill until firm, for 1 hour.

4. Use a tablespoon and scoop out balls from the chilled PB mixture onto the baking sheet or a plate. Shape into a ball using your hands and do the same with all of the PB mixtures. Chill in the freezer or refrigerator and melt the chocolate.

5. Place the coconut oil and chocolate in a liquid measuring cup or a microwave-proof bowl in a microwave. Heat up for 1 minute, take out and mix. If it is not entirely melted, again microwave for 15-second intervals, stirring between each until completely smooth.

6. With a fork, roll each coconut peanut butter ball in the chocolate and drip off any excess chocolate. Then place on a baking sheet or plate -lined with parchment. Sprinkle chopped peanuts or toasted coconut on the balls, if desired.

7. Chill until chocolate is hard, for about 10 minutes. Keeps in the refrigerator for about a month.

4. Chocolate Coconut Almond Fat Bombs

Prep. Time: 10 minutes

Servings: 30 fat bombs

Serving size: 2 fat bombs

Nutrition as per serving

72kcal / 7g fat / 1g carbs / 1g fiber / 0g protein = 0g net carbs

Ingredients

- Cacao powder ¼ cup
- Cacao nibs ¼ cup
- Coconut oil, melted ½ cup
- Coconut Butter melted ½ cup
- Almonds crushed or sliced ¼ cup
- Stevia 10 drops (or erythritol ½ tsp.)
- Almond extracts 1 tsp.
- Vanilla extracts ½ tsp.
- Coconut, unsweetened & finely shredded ¼ cup

Directions

1. Mix coconut butter, coconut oil, cacao powder, vanilla extract, almond extract, erythritol, or stevia. If adding erythritol: heat on the stove or in the microwave for 1 to 2 minutes, it is dissolved. There should be no crunchy erythritol crystals.

2. Mix in the slivered or crushed almonds, cacao nibs and coconut flakes. With the tablespoon's help, fill an ice cube tray or mini cupcake liners, putting one spoonful in each. Keep in the fridge.

5. Mexican Spiced Keto Chocolate

Prep. Time: 10 minute

Servings: 18 pieces

Serving size: 1 piece

Nutrition as per serving

40kcal / 3g fat / 6g carbs / 1g fiber / 3g protein = 5g net carbs

Ingredients

- Cocoa powder 1/2 cup
- Cacao butter melted 1/4 cup
- Nutmeg 1/8 tsp.
- Cinnamon 1/4 tsp.
- Chili powder 1/2 tsp.
- Stevia, 25 drops
- Fine sea salt 1 pinch
- Black pepper 1 pinch
- Vanilla extracts 1/4 tsp.

Directions

1. In a medium mixing bowl, mix the dry ingredients together. Put aside.
2. Melt the cacao butter into a microwave-proof bowl on high for 30-second intervals until melted. Stir in between.
3. To the melted butter, add the stevia and vanilla.
4. Pour this cacao butter mixture into the dry mixture and mix until smooth.
5. Split the mixture between slightly greased baking trays or two loaf pans.
6. Leave it to solidify at room temperature. When set, break into 18 pieces.
7. Keep in a sealed box at room temperature for about 5 days.

6. Chocolate Almond Avocado Pudding Recipe

Prep. Time: 5 minutes

Servings: 3

Serving size: 1 cup

Nutrition as per serving

288 kcal / 14.3g fat / 12g carbs / 8g fiber / 5g protein = 4g net carbs

Ingredients

- Almond milk 1 1/2 cups
- Erythritol blends /granulated stevia 3 tbsp.
- Coconut cream 1/2 cup
- Avocado peeled & pitted medium 1 (6 oz.)
- Almond extracts 1 tsp.
- Cocoa powder unsweetened 3 tbsp.
- Vanilla extracts 1 tsp.
- Almonds sliced for garnish (optional)
- Coconut flakes, unsweetened for garnish (optional)

Directions

1. Blend all the ingredients in a power blender until smooth.
2. Pour into 3 cups, cover and chill for at least 5 hours or, if possible, overnight before serving.
3. Sprinkle sliced almonds and unsweetened coconut flakes before serving.

Chapter 8- 7 Day Sample Meal Plan:

While the keto vegan diet can sound rather restricting, many meals can indeed be produced with vegan-friendly items. Here is a 7-day meal plan with the recipes provided in this cookbook to kick start your keto vegan journey to shed weight.

Monday

- Breakfast: low-carb keto oatmeal
- Lunch: mashed cauliflower with garlic and herbs
- Dinner: easy broccoli soup with vegan arugula avocado salad

Tuesday

- Breakfast: vegan scrambled eggs.
- Lunch: Thai Zucchini noodles with Asian cucumber salad.
- Dinner: cauliflower fried rice with vegan cheese.

Wednesday

- Breakfast: overnight vegan keto Chia pudding
- Lunch: Vegan Thai soup.
- Dinner: Keto mac and cheese with Keto cheese sauce.

Thursday

- Breakfast: tofu shakshuka
- Lunch: lo-carb vegan tahini bowl
- Dinner. Portobello pizza keto stuffed mushrooms.

Friday

- Breakfast: vegan bulletproof coffee and avocado.
- Lunch: creamy tomato soup with oven-roasted lemon garlic asparagus.
- Dinner: Indian baingan bharta with oven-baked healthy zucchini chips.

Saturday

- Breakfast: Vegan keto smoothie with full-fat coconut milk, almond butter, cocoa powder and vegan protein powder.
- Lunch: Low-Carb Shiitake Mushroom Fried Rice.
- Dinner: Cauliflower fried rice with Sunflower Courgetti Seed Cheese.

Sunday

- Breakfast: Vegan keto protein smoothie bowl.
- Lunch: red curry cauliflower soup with Triple green kale salad.
- Dinner: zucchini Alfredo pasta with guacamole and crackers.

Vegan keto snacks

Try these vegan-friendly snacks to hold the hunger in the balance between meals:

- Nuts and coconut bars
- Sliced cucumber and vegan cream cheese spread
- Roasted peanuts or pumpkin seeds
- Guacamole with sliced bell pepper
- Coconut fat bombs (high-fat snacks/dessert made with shredded coconut oil and coconut butter)
- Trail mix with unsweetened coconut mixed nuts, and seeds
- Cocoa smoothie and coconut milk
- Dried unsweetened coconut flakes
- Olives stuffed with vegan cheese
- Celery sticks with almond butter dip
- Cauliflower tater tots
- Coconut cream with berries
- Coconut milk yogurt garnished with chopped almonds

There are so many delicious items to select from when on a vegan keto diet. Snacks and meals should be low in carbs and high in healthy fats.

Conclusion

Having a healthy, illness-free body is the goal for everybody. Physical exercise, a strict nutritious diet and a healthy lifestyle are the best ways to promote good health.

Vegan and Ketogenic diets are two of today's main wellness trends. While these two may not seem like they match together with each other because the vegan diet focuses mostly on a high quantity of carbs as the main source of nourishment, and the Keto diet limits carbs to 20-25g per day. Hence, vegans may still adopt a Ketogenic regimen, enabling them to attain the beneficial effects of each.

The Keto vegan diet is a high-fat, moderate protein, low-carb diet that eliminates all meat and dairy products. Vegetable-based Ketogenic diet ingredients contain vegetables lowest in carbs, almonds and all kinds of nuts and seeds, vegan protein sources, beans, coconut and healthy oils.

Vegans who follow a Vegan Ketogenic diet should consume unprocessed and natural foods in addition to low-carb vegan foods and avoid vegan foods that are highly processed.

High-carb foods like sweetened drinks, grains, and starchy vegetables (like potatoes, peas, turnips), should be eliminated when adopting a vegan-based Ketogenic diet.

Certain minerals and vitamins, including iron and vitamins B12 and vitamin D, should be taken to ensure that nutritional specifications are fulfilled.

High-fat and low-carb diets should not be used during pregnancy, breastfeeding, infancy, or while recovering from such medical conditions. If you are unsure about the Vegan Keto diet is the correct option for you, obtain support and guidance from your physician.

The Complete Ketogenic Guidebook for Women Over 50

Easy Anti-inflammatory Recipes to Lose Belly Fat, Boost your Metabolism, and increase your energy above the age of 50

By
Jamie Carter

Table of contents

Introduction

A Keto diet is one that is very low in carbohydrates but rich in fats and is normal on protein. Through the years, the Keto diet has been used to treat a variety of diseases that people have learned to face. This includes: rectifying weight gain as well as managing or treating diseases of human beings like treating epilepsy in youngsters. The Keto diet enables the human body to use its fats instead of consuming its carbohydrates. Typically, the body's carbohydrates, which are present in the foods you eat, are transformed into glucose. Glucose is a consequence of the body burning off its carbohydrates which are typically distributed throughout the body. A dietary strategy and a balanced lifestyle are, thus, an important necessity for all the citizens who choose to prevent early mortality. Health problems are widely prevalent in women over the age of 50 since they suffer from normal bodily adjustments related to menopause.

Osteoporosis, hypertension, high blood pressure, overweight, and inflammation are popular among women of this category. An effective metabolism is a secret to good health! The level of metabolism does not stay the same, though! As an individual age, the body naturally moves through a slow metabolic phase. This phase of aging speeds up as we eat unhealthy food and live an unhealthy lifestyle, resulting in a variety of metabolic disorders and other associated diseases. It's a popular myth that you'll be consuming bland and fatty food while you're on a ketogenic diet. Although basic foods are a necessity, there are so many ways to bring the spice back into your diet.

Doing keto doesn't just include consuming any type of fat or having ice cream on the mouth. Instead, it's about choosing products that are high in healthy fats and poor in carbohydrates cautiously. If you aren't sure where to go, don't be afraid. Some really good, fantastic keto meals are out there promising to be eaten.

Chapter 1: Introduction to Ketogenic Diet

A ketogenic diet is widely known as a diet which is low in carbs and in which the human body generates ketones to be processed as energy in the liver. Several different names are related to a keto diet, lower-carb diet, lower-carb high fat (LCHF), etc. Patterns of diet come and go, and it seems like the formula mostly includes a low-carb plan. At the top of the chart right now is the ketogenic diet. The keto diet, also referred to as the ketogenic diet, relies on having more of the calories from protein and a few from fat while eliminating carbohydrates dramatically.

1.1 How Does The Ketogenic Diet Work?

A high fat, medium protein, low carbohydrate diet plan, which varies from standard, balanced eating recommendations, is the ketogenic diet. Many foods abundant in nutrients, including vegetables, fruits, whole grains, milk products, are sources of carbohydrates. Carbs from both types are highly constrained on a keto diet. Keto dieters, therefore, do not eat bread, grains, or cereals with the intention of holding carbs below 50 g a day. And since them, too, contain carbohydrates, even fruits and vegetables are restricted. The keto diet involves making drastic changes about how they normally consume for most individuals.

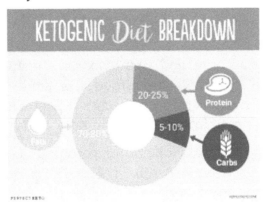

What is Ketosis?

Ketosis is a metabolic condition where the body utilizes fat and ketones as the main source of fuel instead of glucose (sugar).

A critical part of beginning a keto diet is knowing how Ketosis works. Ketosis, irrespective of the number of carbohydrates you consume, is a phase that the body goes through on a daily basis. This is because if sugar is not readily accessible, this method provides humans energy from ketones.

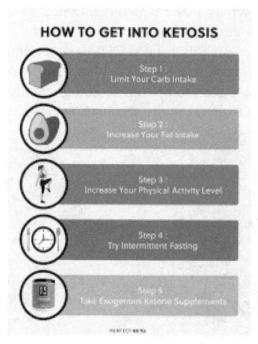

The body tends to raise its ketone levels if the requirement for energy grows, and carbohydrates are not sufficient to satisfy the need. If a more extended period of time (i.e., more than three days) is limited to carbohydrates, the body can raise ketone levels much more. These deeper ketosis rates produce several favorable benefits in the body, results that are achieved when adopting the ketogenic diet is the best and healthiest manner practicable.

Most individuals, however, seldom get Ketosis and never feel its advantages because the body tends to use sugar as its main source of power, even if the diet provides plenty of carbohydrates and protein.

How does Ketosis happen?

The body would turn any of its accumulated fat into extremely effective energy molecules called ketones while the body has no access to healthy food, like while you are resting, exercising, or adopting a ketogenic diet. (We should credit our body's capacity to alter metabolic processes for that.) After the body breaks down fat into glycerol and fatty acids, such ketones are synthesized.

While in certain cells in the body, fatty acids and glycerol may be directly converted into food, brain cells do not use them as energy at all. This really is because they are so gradually processed into energy to help the brain work.

That's why sugar appears to be the brain's primary source of fuel. Interestingly, this also enables one to realize that we make ketones. Thus providing an alternate source of energy, because we do not eat sufficient calories, our brain will be incredibly susceptible. Our muscles will be quickly broken down and transformed into glucose to support our brains that are sugar-hungry before we have enough power left to find food. The human species would most definitely be endangered without ketones.

1.2 Types of Ketogenic Diet

There are a variety of aspects in which ketosis can be induced, and so there are a number of diverse ketogenic diet variations.

Keto Diet Standard (SKD)

This is a really low carb diet, a medium protein diet yet high fat. Usually, it comprises 70 to 75% fat, 20% protein, and only 5 to 10% carbohydrates.

A traditional standard ketogenic diet, in terms of grams per day, will be:

- Carbohydrate between 20-50g

- Around 40-60g of protein

- No limit specified for fat

The bulk of calories should be given by fat in the diet for this to be a keto diet. As energy needs might differ greatly among individuals, no limit is set. A large number of vegetables, especially non-starchy veggies, should be included in ketogenic diets, as they are very low in carbs.

In order to help people reduce weight, increase blood glucose regulation and improve cardiac health, standardized ketogenic diets have repeatedly demonstrated success.

Very-low-carb diet ketogenic (VLCKD)

Very-low-carb is a traditional ketogenic diet, and so a VLCKD would normally correspond to a traditional ketogenic diet.

Ketogenic Diet Well Formulated (WFKD)

The word 'Well Formulated Keto Diet' derives from one of the main ketogenic diet experts, Steve Phinney.

As a traditional ketogenic diet, the WFKD maintains a similar blueprint. Well-developed ensures that weight, protein & carbohydrate macronutrients align with the ratios of the traditional ketogenic diet and thus have the greatest likelihood of ketosis happening.

Ketogenic Diet MCT

This fits the description of the traditional ketogenic diet but insists on providing more of the diet's fat content through the use of medium-chain triglycerides (MCTs). MCTs are present in coconut oil and are accessible in the liquid state of MCT oil and MCT dispersant.

To treat epilepsy, MCT ketogenic diets are being used since the idea is that MCTs enable individuals to absorb more carbohydrates and protein, thus sustaining ketosis. That's because multiple ketones per gram of fat are produced by MCTs than the long-chain triglycerides found in natural dietary fat. There is a dearth of research, though, exploring whether MCTs have greater advantages on weight loss and blood sugar.

Ketogenic diet Calorie-restricted

Unless calories are reduced to a fixed number, a calorie-restricted ketogenic diet is identical to a normal ketogenic diet.

Research indicates that, whether calorie consumption is reduced or not, ketogenic diets seem to be effective. This is because it helps to avoid over-eating of itself from the nutritious impact of eating fat and staying in ketosis.

The Ketogenic Cyclical Diet (CKD)

There are days on which more carbohydrates are ingested, like five ketogenic days accompanied by two high carbohydrate days, in the CKD diet, frequently recognized as carb back loading.

The diet is meant for athletes who can regenerate glycogen drained from muscles during exercises using the high carbohydrate days.

Ketogenic Diet Targeted (TKD)

Even though carbs are eaten around exercise hours, the TKD is equivalent to a typical ketogenic diet. It is a combination between a regular ketogenic diet as well as a cyclical ketogenic diet that requires every day you work out to eat carbohydrates.

It is focused on the assumption that carbohydrates eaten before or during a physical effort can be absorbed even more effectively, while the need for energy from the muscles rises while we are engaged.

Ketogenic Diet of High Protein

With a proportion of 35 percent protein, 60 percent fat, and 5 percent carbohydrates, this diet contains more protein than a regular keto diet.

For people who need to lose weight, a study shows that a high-protein keto is beneficial for weight loss. Like in other types of the ketogenic diet, if practiced for several years, there is an absence of research on which there are any health risks.

1.3 Benefits of Ketogenic Diet

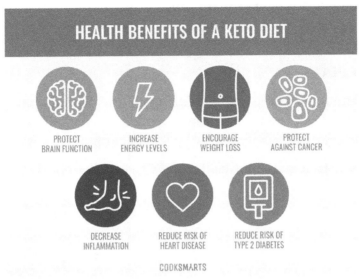

A keto diet has many advantages, including:

Weight Reduction

A person's keto diet will help them lose weight. The keto diet help encourages weight loss in many aspects, particularly metabolism boosting and appetite reduction. Ketogenic diets comprise foods that load up an individual and can minimize hormones that trigger appetite. For these factors, it may suppress appetite and encourage weight loss by adopting a keto diet.

Helps improve acne

In certain persons, acne has many common reasons and can have associations with diet and blood sugar. Consuming a diet rich in highly processed carbs can change the equivalence of intestinal bacteria and cause major rises and declines in blood sugar, both of which would negatively impact the health of the skin.

It can decrease the risk of certain cancers.

The implications of the ketogenic diet have been studied by experts to potentially avoid or even cure some cancers. One research showed that in patients with some cancers, a ketogenic diet could be a healthy and appropriate complementary medication to be used in addition to chemotherapy and radiation therapy. This is because, in cancer cells, it might cause greater oxidative stress than in regular cells, allowing them to die.

It can safeguard brain function.

Some research indicates that neuroprotective advantages are offered by the ketones developed during the ketogenic diet that indicates they can reinforce and defend the brain and nerve cells.

A ketogenic diet might help a person resist or maintain problems such as Alzheimer's disease for this purpose.

Lessens seizures potentially

In a ketogenic diet, the proportion of fat, protein, and carbohydrates changes the way the body utilizes energy, results in ketosis. Ketosis is a biochemical mechanism in which ketone bodies are being used by the body for energy.

The Epilepsy Foundation indicates that ketosis in people with epilepsy, particularly those who have not adapted to other types of treatment, might decrease seizures. More study is required on how efficient this is, as it seems to have the greatest influence on children who have generalized seizures.

Improves the effects of PCOS

Polycystic ovary syndrome (PCOS) may contribute to surplus male hormones, ovulatory instability, and polycystic ovaries as a hormonal syndrome. In individuals with PCOS, a high-carbohydrate diet can trigger negative impacts, like skin problems as well as excess weight.

The researchers observed that many markers of PCOS are strengthened by a ketogenic diet, including:

- Loss in weight
- Balance of hormones
- Ratios of follicle-stimulating hormone (LH) and luteinizing hormone (LH) (FSH)
- Insulin fasting levels

A different research analysis showed that for people with hormonal conditions, like PCOS and type 2 diabetes, a keto diet has positive benefits. They also cautioned, though, that the findings were too diverse to prescribe a keto diet as a specific PCOS treatment.

Chapter 2: Easy ketogenic Low Carb Recipes

It may be challenging to adopt different diets: all the foods to quit, to consume more, to purchase new products. It's enough to make bonkers for everyone. But the ketogenic, or "keto," diet, as well as its keto meals, are one type of eating that has been gathering traction lately.

Doing keto doesn't only involve eating some sort of fat or putting ice cream on your mouth. Rather, it's about picking items that are rich in good fats and low in carbohydrates carefully. If you aren't sure where to start, don't be scared. Some very healthy, excellent keto meals are out there appealing to be consumed.

2.1 Keto Breakfast Recipes

1. HIGH PROTEIN COTTAGE CHEESE OMELET

Serving: 1

Preparation time: 5 minutes

Nutritional Values: 250kcal Calories | 18g Fat | 4 g Carbs | 18.7g Proteins

Ingredients

- 2 eggs - large
- 1 tbsp. of whole milk or 2% milk
- Kosher salt about 1/8 tsp.
- Pinch of black pepper, freshly ground,
- 1/2 tbsp. of butter - unsalted
- 1 cup spinach (about 1 ounce)
- Cottage cheese 3 tbsp.

Directions

1. In a moderate pan, put the eggs, milk, salt, & pepper and stir until the whites & yolks are thoroughly combined, and the eggs are a little viscous.

2. In an 8-inch non - stick roasting pan over medium heat, add the butter. Flip the pan until the butter covers the bottom equally. Include the spinach and simmer for around 30 seconds before it is ripened. Put the eggs in and turn the pan directly so that the eggs cover the whole bottom.

3. To softly pull and move the cooked eggs from the sides into the middle of the pan, use either a silicone or rubber spatula, leaving room for the raw eggs and creating waves in the omelet. Rig a spatula underneath the edges to enable raw eggs to run beneath the cooked part, holding and swiveling the pan. Cook for around 2 minutes until the sides are settled, and the middle is moist but no longer soft or gooey.

4. Let the pan away from the heat. Whisk over half the eggs with the cottage cheese. Cover the egg carefully over the filling using a spatula. On a plate, transfer the omelet.

2. DEVILED EGGS

Serving: 4-6

Preparation time: 15-20 minutes

Nutritional values: 280kcal Calories | 23g Fat | 3.4g Carbs | 15g Proteins

Ingredients

- 12 eggs - large
- 8 oz. of full-fat cream cheese, warmed for 1 hour or more at room temperature,
- Kosher salt about 1/2 teaspoon
- 1 shred of black pepper
- 2 tablespoons of all the bagel seasoning

Directions

1. A dozen eggs become hardboiled according to your chosen method. (The most critical part is to layer with ice water, raise to a boil, then lift from the heat and leave for 8 to 10 minutes to remain.) In an ice bucket, soak and chill the eggs. And peel them.

2. Cut the eggs laterally in half and use a tiny spoon to pick the yolks out and put them in a dish.

3. Take the cream cheese and transfer it to the yolks into rough parts. Use a hand beater or stick mixer to mix until smooth and blended, starting at lower speeds and then at high speed. Bang in the pepper and salt. Uh, taste. If needed, tweak the seasonings.

4. Load the egg whites with the yolk mixture using a spoon or piping bag. (It would be stiff; to soften it any further if possible, microwave it in very fast bursts of 2 to 3 seconds.)

5. With the all-bagel seasoning, dust the tops of the loaded eggs appropriately. In two hours, serve.

3. 90 SECOND KETO BREAD

Serving: 1

Preparation time: 90 seconds

Nutritional values: 99kcal Calories | 8.5g Fat | 2g Carbs | 3.9g Proteins

Instructions

- 1 egg - large
- 1 spoonful of milk
- Olive oil about 1 tablespoon
- 1 tablespoon flour of coconut
- 1 tablespoon flour of almonds or hazelnuts
- 1/4 tsp. powder for baking
- Pinch of salt

Add-ins optional:

- 1/4 cup of grated cheese
- 1 tbsp. scallions or herbs chopped

Directions

1. In a small cup, mix together the egg, milk, oil, coconut flour, almond flour, baking powder, and salt. If using, incorporate cheese and scallions or herbs and mix to blend.

2. To induce any air bubbles to lift and burst, pour into a wide microwave-safe mug and strike the bottom tightly on the counter multiple times. Reheat for 1 minute, 30 seconds, on maximum.

3. On a chopping board, transpose the mug and enable the bread to drop out. Slice into 1/2-inch-thick strips crosswise. For the toast, heat a teaspoon of oil across moderate flame in a small pan until it glistens. Add the strips and toast, around 30 seconds on either side, before golden-brown.

4. KETO FRITTATA

Serving: 4-6

Preparation time: 25 minutes

Nutritional values: 155kcal Calories | 8.9g Fat | 11.4g Carbs | 7.9g Proteins

Instructions

- 6 large eggs, sufficient for the ingredients to fill
- Heavy cream 1/4 cup
- 1 tsp. of kosher salt, split-up
- 4 thick-cut bacon (8 oz.) pieces, diced (optional)
- 2 tiny, stripped, and finely diced Yukon gold potatoes
- 1/4 tsp. of black pepper, freshly ground
- 2 cups of spinach (2 ounces)
- Garlic 2 cloves, chopped.
- 2 tsp. of fresh leaves of thyme
- 1 cup of Gruyere, Fontina, or Cheddar crushed cheese

Directions

1. Preheat oven. In the center of the oven, position a brace and warm it to 400 °F.

2. Stir together the cream and eggs. In a medium bowl, stir together the eggs, whipping cream, and 1/2 teaspoon salt; hold.

3. Just prepare the bacon. Put the bacon in a non - stick 10-12-inch cold cooking pan or cast-iron skillet, and keep the heat to moderate. Cook the bacon until translucent, stirring regularly, for 8 to 10 minutes. Move the bacon to a paper towel-lined dish with a slotted spoon and skim off all but 2 tbsp. of the fat. (If the bacon is excluded, heat the pan with 2 tablespoons of oil, then finish incorporating the potatoes).

4. Simmer the potatoes in the fat of the bacon. Mix the potatoes and spray with the pepper and the remaining 1/2 teaspoon salt. Switch the pan to a moderate flame. Heat, stirring regularly, for 4 to 6 minutes, until soft and golden brown.

5. Crumble the spinach with thyme & garlic. Put the spinach, garlic, and thyme in the pan and cook, mixing, for 30 seconds to 1 minute, or until the spinach is wilted. Transfer the bacon again to the skillet and swirl to spread uniformly.

6. Add some cheese. Scattered the vegetables, compressed with a spatula, into an even layer. Over the top, spread the cheese and let it only begin to melt.

7. In the pan, add the egg mixture. Place over the vegetables and cheese with the egg mixture. To be sure that the eggs settle equally over all the vegetables, rotate the skillet. Wait for a minute or two before you observe the eggs starting to set at the ends of the pan.

8. Around 8 to 10 minutes, oven the frittata. Bake for 8 to 10 minutes unless the eggs are ready. Cut a tiny slit in the middle of the frittata to test. Bake for a few more minutes if uncooked eggs run into the cut; if the eggs are fixed, take the frittata out of the oven. At the end of cooking, hold the frittata underneath the broiler for a couple of minutes for a crisped, charred layer.

9. For 5 minutes, chill in the skillet, then cut into slices and serve.

5. CHEESE, HAM, AND EGG WRAPS

Serving: 4

Preparation time: 15-20 minutes

Nutritional values: 371kcal calories | 27g Fat | ‰g Carbs | 27g Proteins

Ingredients

- 8 eggs - large
- 4 tsp. of Water
- 2 tsp. of all-purpose or cornstarch flour
- Half a teaspoon of fine salt
- 4 tsp. of coconut or vegetable oil
- 1 1/3 cups of Swiss grated cheese
- 4 ounces of ham extremely thinly sliced
- 1 1/3 cups of watercress loosely wrapped

Directions

1. In a wide bowl, put the eggs, water, flour or cornflour, and salt, and stir until the starch or cornflour is fully dissolved.

2. In a 12-inch non - stick saucepan, heat 1 tsp. Of oil unless glinting, over moderate flame. To cover the surface with the oil, move the pan. To brush the bottom part in a thin coating, incorporate 1/2 cup of the egg mixture and stir. Cook for 3 to 6 minutes before the wrapping is fully set on the sides and on the surface (the top may be a little damp but should be apparently set).

3. Soften the sides of the wrap using a wide spatula and move it under the wrap, ensuring that it will slide across the pan quickly. With the spatula, turn the wrap. Slather 1/3 cup of cheese instantly over the wrap and simmer for around 1 minute before the second side is ready. Drop it onto a chopping board or work surface (the cheese may not be completely melted yet). Put a single coat of ham over the egg when it is still hot. Put 1/3 of a cup of watercress in the middle of the wrap. Firmly roll it up.

4. Repeat the leftover wraps by cooking and filling them. Slice each wrap crosswise into 6 (1-inch) bits using a steak knife.

6. BACON GRUYERE EGG BITES

Serving: 9

Preparation time: 10-20 minutes

Nutritional values: 208kcal Calories | 18g Fat | 1g Carbs | 11g Proteins

Ingredients

- Fat or butter of bacon, to coat the pan
- 9 large eggs
- 3/4 cup Gruyere cheese grated (2 1/4 oz.)
- 1/3 cup (about 2 1/2 oz.) cream cheese
- Kosher salt about 1/2 teaspoon
- 6 pieces of thick-cut, cooked, and imploded bacon

Directions

1. In the center of the oven, place a rack and warm it to 350°F. Graciously cover an 8x8-inch (broiler-safe if you like a crisped top) cooking dish with bacon fat or butter.

2. Put the eggs, Gruyere, cream cheese, and salt in a mixer and combine for around 1 minute, at moderate speed, until quite smooth. Drop it into the pan for baking. Slather bacon with it. With aluminum foil, cover firmly.

3. Take the oven rack out from the oven midway. Upon on the oven rack, put a roasting tray. Put in 6 extremely hot tap water pots. Place the baking dish in the hot skillet with the eggs. Bake until the center is just ready, 55 minutes to 1 hour.

4. Pull the roasting pan from the oven cautiously. Remove the roasting pan from the baking dish and unfold it. (For a browned surface: Heat the oven to sauté. Sauté 4 to 5 minutes before the top is golden-brown.) Slice and serve into 9 squares.

7. RADISH TURNIP AND FRIED EGGS HASH WITH GREEN GARLIC

Serving: 2

Preparation time: 10-12 minutes

Nutritional values: 392kcal calories | 34g Fat | 10g Carbs | 13g Proteins

Ingredients

- 2 to 3 tiny turnips (approximately 1 1/2 cups cubed) clipped, peeled, and sliced into 3/4-inch cubes
- 4 to 5 tiny, rinsed and clipped radishes, and sliced into 3/4-inch cubes (approximately 1 1/2 cubed cups)
- Crushed Salt of the Sea
- Pepper freshly crushed
- 2 tbsp. of grapeseed oil, or other heat-tolerant, neutral oil
- 1 green garlic stalk, clipped and diced (just white and light green parts)
- 2 spoonful's of unsalted butter
- Four eggs
- 1 tablespoon parsley chopped

Directions

1. Place the water in a wide skillet and raise it to a boil. Stir in 2 teaspoons of sea salt. Transfer to a bowl with a slotted spoon, skim off any extra water and set it aside. Simmer turnip cubes only until moist, 3 to 4 minutes. Next, quickly boil the radishes for 30 to 60 seconds; scrape with a slotted spoon in a pan, skim off any extra water, and set it aside.

2. Place a sauté pan of cast iron over moderate flame. Include the grapeseed oil and add the turnips & radishes when warm, and pinch the sea salt and pepper with each one. Cook for 8 minutes or until golden-brown, flipping vegetables just once or twice. Switch the heat to medium, bring in the green garlic and simmer for a minute or so. Place the vegetables to the edges, melt the butter in the center of the pan, and add the eggs. Cook unearthed for 4 to 6 minutes for over-easy eggs; close pan for 3 minutes for over-medium

eggs, then unfold and continue to cook only until whites are ready, 2 to 3 minutes further. To taste, finish with chopped parsley and sea salt and pepper. Instantly serve.

8. CAULIFLOWER RICE BURRITO BOWLS

Serving: 4

Preparation time: 20-25 minutes

Nutritional values: 374kcal Calories | 15g Fat | 46g Carbs | 21g Protein

Ingredients

- 1 (15-ounce) canned washed and cleaned black beans.
- 1 cup of corn kernels - frozen
- 2 spoonful's of water
- Chili powder about 1/2 teaspoon
- 1/2 teaspoon of cumin powder
- 3/4 teaspoon of kosher salt, distributed
- 1 tablespoon of olive oil
- One cauliflower of a medium head (just around 1 1/2 lbs.), riced (or one 16oz sack riced cauliflower)
- 1/3 cup of fresh cilantro minced, distributed
- 1/4 cup of lime juice, freshly extracted (from 2 to 3 lemons)
- 1 cup roasted chicken chopped or shredded (optional), warmed if necessary
- 1 cup of gallo pico de or salsa
- One large, drained, pitted, and diced avocado

Directions

1. In a small pan, put the beans, corn, water, chili powder, cumin, and 1/4 tsp. over moderate flame. Cook for 3 to 5 minutes, mixing periodically until hot. Distance yourself from the steam.

2. In the meantime, over a moderate flame, heat the oil in a wide, large skillet until it shimmers. Transfer the cauliflower and the residual 1/2 teaspoon salt to the mixture.

Process until the cauliflower is cooked through though soft, 3 to 5 minutes, mixing periodically. Remove from the heat. Transfer the cilantro and lime juice to 1/4 cup and mix to blend.

3. Divide into four bowls the riced cauliflower. Cover with the mixture of bean and corn, chicken if used, pico de gallo or salsa, and pieces of avocado. Slather with the cilantro that persists and serve hot.

9. KETO LOAF

Serving: 1

Preparation time: 10-12 minutes

Nutritional values: 239kcal Calories | 22g Fat | 4g carbs | 8g Proteins

Ingredients

- Two cups of fine powdered almond flour, especially brands like King Arthur
- 1 tsp. powder for baking
- 1/2 tsp. of gum xanthan
- Kosher salt about 1\2 tsp.
- 7 eggs - large
- 8 tbsp. (1 stick) of melted and chilled unsalted butter
- 2 tbsp. of concentrated, processed, and chilled coconut oil

Directions

1. In the center of the oven, place a rack and warm it to 351°F. Cover the bottom part of a parchment paper 9x5-inch metallic loaf pan, having the surplus spill around the long sides to create a loop. Just set aside.

2. In a wide dish, mix together the flour of almond, powder for baking, xanthan gum, as well as salt. Just placed back.

3. Put the eggs in a bowl equipped with the whisk extension of a stand blender. Beat at moderate pressure until soft and drippy. Lower the level to moderate, incorporate the butter and oil of coconut gradually, and whisk unless well mixed. Lessen the intensity to

medium, incorporate the mixture of almond flour gradually, and mix unless mixed. Rise the pace to moderate and beat for around 1 minute before the mixture thickens.

4. Pour and scrape the top into the primed pan. Bake for 45 to 55 minutes unless a knife placed in the middle comes out clean. Let it cool for around ten minutes in the pan. Take the loaf over the skillet, grab the parchment paper, and shift it to a cutting board. Cool it down completely until slicing.

10. BREAKFAST SALAD

Serving: 4

Preparation time: 10 minutes

Nutritional values: 425kcal Calories | 34g Fat | 16g Carbs | 17g Proteins

Ingredients

- Spinach 8 Oz (about 6 packed cups)
- 1/2 a cup of blueberries
- 1 medium-sized avocado, chopped
- 1/3 cup red roasted quinoa
- 1/4 cup of pumpkin seeds - toasted
- Bacon - 6 strips
- 4 eggs of large size
- 1/4 cup of apple cider vinegar
- 2 tsp. of honey
- Kosher salt about 1\2 tsp.

Directions

1. In a large bowl, add the spinach, avocado, berries, pumpkin seeds, and quinoa and toss them to mix. Distribute the salad into deep plates or pots.

2. Put the bacon over moderate heat in a large cast-iron pan. Cook until the fat has dried out and the bacon is crunchy, tossing halfway around for a total of around 10 minutes. Shift

the bacon to a tray that is lined with paper towels. Cut the bacon into little crumbles until it is cold.

3. Lower the heat and fry the eggs to the perfect braising in the dried bacon fat. Keep the pan away from the heat. Place the toppled bacon and an egg on top of each salad.

4. Upon emulsification, mix the vinegar, honey, and salt into the residual bacon fat in the dish. Sprinkle over the salad with the warm dressing and serve promptly.

2.2 Keto Lunch & Dinner Recipes

1. CAULIFLOWER FRIED RICE

Serving: 4

Preparation time: 20- 25 minutes

Nutritional values: 108kcal Calories | 1g Fat | 21g Carbs | 7g Proteins

Ingredients

For Fried Rice

- 1 cauliflower head, sliced into cloves
- Balanced Oil 2 tbsp. (such as vegetable, coconut, or peanut)
- 1 bunch of finely sliced scallions
- 3 cloves of garlic, chopped
- 1 tbsp. natural ginger diced
- 2 peeled and finely chopped carrots
- 2 stalks of celery, chopped
- 1 bell pepper, red, chopped
- 1 cup of peas - frozen
- 2 tbsp. vinegar for rice
- 3 spoonful's of soy sauce
- Sriracha 2 tsp., or enough to taste

For Garnishing

- Balanced oil about 1tbsp. (such as vegetable, coconut, or peanut)
- Four eggs

- Salt and black pepper finely processed
- 4 tbsp. of fresh cilantro, diced
- 4 tbsp. of scallions thinly diced
- 4 tsp. of seeds of sesame

Directions

1. **For Fried Rice:** Pump the cauliflower in the mixing bowl for 2 or 3 minutes before the mishmash resembles rice. Just set aside.

2. Heat oil over a moderate flame in a wide skillet. Include the scallions, garlic, and ginger and mix for around 1 minute, unless aromatic.

3. Incorporate the carrots, celery & red bell pepper, and braise for 9 to 11 minutes until the veggies are soft.

4. Add the cauliflower rice, then stir-fry for another 3 to 5 minutes, once it starts to turn golden. To blend, mix in the frozen peas and toss properly.

5. To combine, incorporate rice vinegar, Sriracha, and soy sauce & swirl. Just set aside.

6. **For Garnishing:** Add the oil in a large skillet over moderate to high flame. Crack the eggs straight into the skillet and stir for 3 to 4 minutes before the whites are assertive, but the yolks are still watery. With pepper and salt, sprinkle each one.

7. Distribute the cauliflower rice into four dishes to serving and serve each one with a fried egg. Sprinkle with 1 tablespoon of cilantro, 1 tablespoon of scallions, and 1 teaspoon of sesame seeds on each dish. Instantly serve then.

2. LOW CARB THAI CURRY SOUP

Serving: 6

Preparation time: 22 minutes

Nutritional values: 324kcal Calories | 27g Fat | 7g Carbs | 15g Proteins

Ingredients

- 4 Leg pieces of boneless skinless chicken,

- 14.5 ounces (411.07 g) full-fat coconut milk
- 2 tsp. of Thai paste of yellow curry
- 2 tsp. of fish sauce
- Three tsp. of Soy Sauce
- 1 tsp. of Agave or honey nectar
- 2 green Scallions minced
- Garlic 4 cloves, minced
- 2 inch (2 inches) coarsely chopped diced ginger

Veggies to add in soup

- One Can of Straw Mushrooms (optional)
- 74.5 g (1/2 cup) of Cherry Tomatoes, half-sliced
- Cilantro, 1/4 cup (4 g), diced
- 3 green Scallions diced
- 1 lime, juiced

Directions

For the Instant Pot

1. Put the essential soup components and lock in an Instant Pot.

2. Process it under heat for 12 minutes by using the SOUP key. The soup button avoids it from boiling and extracting the coconut milk.

3. Discharge the pressure immediately and detach and cut the chicken. Place it in the broth again.

4. Transfer the warm broth to the vegetables. In the hot broth, you want to bring them a little scorching but not to mold them though you can actually taste the flavor of the vegetables and herbs.

For the Slow Cooker

1. In a slow cooker, put the essential soup ingredients and steam for 8 hours on lower or 4 hours on average.

2. Over the last half-hour, place in vegetables and herbs. In the hot broth, you want to bring them a little scorching but not to mold them though you can actually taste the flavor of the vegetables and herbs.

3. Remove the chicken and cut it. Place it in the broth again.

- It's actually cheaper to purchase Thai Yellow Curry Paste than to prepare it. At your nearest Asian food store, you will find it.

- With the provided directions, prepare this in your Instant Pot or slow cooker. If required, you may use heavy whipping cream for coconut milk.

3. JALAPENO POPPER SOUP

Serving: 3

Preparation time: 25 minutes

Nutritional values: 446kcal Calories | 35g Fat | 4g Carbs | 28g Proteins

Ingredients

- 4 bacon strips
- 2 spoonful's of butter
- Medium-sized 1/2 onion, chopped
- 1/4 cup of pickled, diced jalapenos
- 2 cups broth of chicken
- 2 cups of shredded chicken, cooked
- Cream cheese 4 ounces
- Heavy cream 1/3 cup
- 1 cup of Fresh Cheddar Shredded
- 1/4 tsp. powdered garlic
- Pepper and salt, to taste
- If needed, 1/2 tsp. xanthan gum for thick soup [Optional]

Directions

1. Fry the bacon in a pan. Crumble when cooked and put aside. Place a large pot over the moderate flame while the bacon cooks. Include the onion and butter and simmer until the onion becomes porous.

2. Transfer the jalapenos and half the crumbled bacon to the pot.

3. Pour in the broth of the chicken and the shredded chicken. Take to a boil, then cook for 20 minutes, and reduce.

4. Put the cream cheese in a medium bowl and microwave for around 20 seconds; once soft until smooth, mix. Stir the cream cheese and the heavy cream into the soup. It may take a few minutes for the cream cheese to be completely integrated. Turn the heat off.

5. Include the shredded cheese, and whisk until it is completely melted. Add xanthan gum at this stage if the thick soup is preferred.

6. Serve with the leftover bacon on top.

4. PEPPERS & SAUSAGES

Serving: 6

Preparation time: 2 hrs.5 minutes

Nutritional values: 313kcal Calories | 22g Fat | 11g Carbs | 16g Proteins

Ingredients

- 1 tablespoon olive oil
- Six medium links of Pork sausage
- 3 of the large Bell peppers (cut into strips)
- 1 onion of large size (cut into half, the same size as the pepper shreds)
- Garlic 6 Cloves (minced)
- 1 tbsp. seasoning Italian
- Sea salt about 1/2 tsp.
- Black pepper 1/4 teaspoon
- 1 and a half cups of Marinara sauce

Directions

1. To activate a kitchen timer whilst you cook, toggle on the times in the directions below.

2. Heat the oil over moderate heat in a large pan. Include the sausage links until its warm. Cook on either side for around 2 minutes, only until golden brown on the outer side. (Inside, they will not be prepared.)

3. In the meantime, in a slow cooker, add the bell peppers, onions, garlic, Italian spices, salt, & pepper. Toss it to coat it. Softly spill the marinara sauce over the veggies.

4. Once the sausage links are golden brown, put them on top of the veggies in the slow cooker.

5. Cook on low flame or 2-3 hours on high flame for 4-5 hours, unless the sausages are cooked completely.

5. SHRIMPS WITH CAULIFLOWER GRITS AND ARUGULA

Serving: 4

Preparation time: 25-30 minutes

Nutritional values: 123kcal Calories | 5g Fat | 3g Carbs | 16g proteins

Ingredients

For Spicy Shrimp

- 1 pound of cleaned and roasted shrimp
- 1 tablespoon of paprika
- 2 teaspoons of powdered garlic
- 1/2 tsp. of pepper cayenne
- 1 tablespoon of olive oil extra virgin
- Salt and black pepper freshly processed
- GRITS of CAULIFLOWER
- Unsalted butter about 1 tablespoon
- Riced cauliflower about four cups
- 1cup of milk
- 1/2 cup of goat's crushed cheese
- Salt & black pepper freshly processed

For Garlic Arugula

- 1 tablespoon of olive oil extra virgin
- 3 cloves of garlic, finely minced
- 4 cups of baby arugula
- Salt & black pepper freshly processed

Directions

1. **Prepare the Spicy Shrimp:** Put the shrimp in a big plastic zip-top pack. Mix the paprika in a tiny bowl with the garlic powder as well as the cayenne to blend. Place the mixture with the shrimp into the packet and shake well before the spices have covered them. Refrigerate the grits while preparing them.

2. **Prepare the Cauliflower "Grits":** Melt the butter over a moderate flame in a wide bowl. Integrate the cauliflower rice and simmer for 2 to 3 minutes once it sheds some of its steam.

3. Whisk in half the milk and raise it to a boil. Continue to boil, stirring regularly, for 6 to 8 minutes, before some milk is consumed by the cauliflower.

4. Add the leftover milk and boil for another 10 minutes before the mixture is smooth and fluffy. Mix in the cheese from the goat and add salt and pepper. Just hold warm.

5. **Prepare Garlic Arugula:** Warm olive oil over moderate heat in a large pan. Add the garlic and simmer for 1 minute unless tangy. Include the arugula and simmer for 3 to 4 minutes, unless softened. Use salt and pepper to season, take from the pan, and put aside.

6. Heat the olive oil over low heat in the same pan. Include shrimp and simmer for 4 to 5 minutes until completely cooked. Use salt and pepper to season.

7. Divide the grits into four dishes to serve, then top each one with a fourth of the arugula & a quarter of the shrimp. Immediately serve.

6. CHICKEN CHILI WHITE

Serving: 4

Preparation time: 35-45 minutes

Nutritional values: 481kcal Calories | 30g Fat | 5g Carbs | 39g Proteins

Ingredients

- 1 lb. breast of chicken
- Chicken broth about 1.5 cups
- 2 cloves of garlic, thinly chopped
- 1 can of sliced green chills
- 1 jalapeno sliced
- 1 green pepper chopped
- 1/4 cup onion finely chopped
- Four tablespoons of butter
- 1/4 cup of heavy whipped cream
- Four-ounce cream cheese
- 2 teaspoons of cumin
- 1 teaspoon of oregano
- Cayenne 1/4 teaspoon (additional)
- To taste: salt & black pepper

Directions

1. Season the chicken with cumin, cayenne, oregano, salt, and black pepper in a wide pan.
2. Braise both sides unless golden, under medium-high heat,

3. Transfer the broth to the pan, cover, and cook for 15-20 minutes or until the chicken is completely cooked.

4. Melt the butter in a moderate pan while the chicken is frying.

5. In the pan, incorporate the chills, chopped jalapeno, green pepper, and onion, and simmer until the vegetables soften.

6. Add the chopped garlic and simmer for an extra 30 seconds, switching off the heat and put aside.

7. When the chicken is fully done, slice it with a fork and transfer it to the broth.

8. In a chicken & broth pan, incorporate the sautéed veggies and cook for 10 minutes.

9. Soften the cream cheese in the microwave in a mixing bowl so you can blend it (~20 sec)

10. Mix the cream cheese and heavy whipped cream

11. Add the mixture of chicken and vegetables into the pot and whisk rapidly.

12. Simmer for an extra 15 minutes.

13. Serve with preferred toppings such as cheese from the pepper jack, slices of avocado, coriander, sour cream.

7. BOWL OF CHICKEN ENCHILADA

Serving: 4

Preparation time: 40-50 minutes

Nutritional values: 570kcal Calories | 40g Fat | 6g Carbs | 38g Proteins

Ingredients

- 2 spoonful's of coconut oil (for searing chicken)
- 1 pound of chicken thighs that are boneless, skinless
- 3/4 cup sauce of red enchilada
- 1/4 of a cup of water

- 1/4 cup onion, minced
- 1-4 oz. green chills Can - sliced

Toppings

- 1 Avocado, sliced
- 1 cup of cheese, crushed
- 1/4 cup of pickled jalapenos, diced
- 1/2 of a cup of sour cream
- 1 tomato Roma, diced

Directions

1. Heat up the coconut oil on a moderate flame in a pan or a Dutch oven. Braise the chicken thighs unless finely brown when hot.

2. Place in the enchilada sauce as well as the water. After this, add the onion and also the green chilies. Lower the heat to a boil and cover it. Cook the chicken for 17-25 minutes or until the chicken is juicy and heated to an inner temperature of approximately 165 degrees.

3. Remove the chicken cautiously and put it on a chopping board. Then put it back into the pot. Cut or shred chicken (your preference). To retain flavor, let the chicken boil uncovered for an extra 10 minutes and enable the sauce to minimize some more.

4. For serving, cover with avocado, cheese, jalapeno, tomato, sour cream, or any other toppings you want. Feel free to adjust them to your taste. If preferred, serve individually or over cauliflower rice; just refresh your personal nutrition details as required.

8. CHIPOTLE HEALTHY KETO PULLED PORK

Serving: 10

Preparation time: 8 hrs.15 minutes

Nutritional values: 430kcal Calories | 34g Fat | 3g Carbs | 27g Proteins

Ingredients

- 1 Mid-yellow onion chopped
- 1 cup of water
- 2 tablespoons of fresh garlic diced
- 1 tablespoon of Coconut Sugar
- 1 tablespoon of salt
- 1 teaspoon of chili powder
- 1/2 teaspoon of cumin powder
- 1/2 Tablespoon Adobo sauce
- Smoked paprika 1/4 teaspoons
- 3 1/2-4 lbs. pork shoulder, Extra fat should be removed
- Whole wheat or hamburger buns without gluten OR salad wraps for serving
- Paleo ranch, to be garnished
- Coleslaw blend for optional garnish
- Lime Juice, to be garnished
- Green Tabasco for garnishing

Directions

1. Cut the onion and chop the garlic, and put it in the base of the slow cooker—a spill in a cup of water.
2. In a small bowl, mix all the ingredients for the seasoning and set it aside.
3. Slice off the pork shoulder some large, noticeable parts of fat and spread it all over with the seasoning until it is uniformly covered.
4. Over the top of the garlic, onions & water, add the pork and simmer until soft and juicy, 6-8 hours on maximum or 8-10 hours on reduced.
5. If the pork is cooked, extract much of the liquid from the crockpot and put the solids directly into the crockpot (which comprises the garlic and onions).
6. On a chopping board, move the pork and slice it with two forks.
7. In the slow cooker, shift the sliced pork back and combine with the onions and garlic. Cover unless ready to be served, and keep it warm.
8. On a bun or lettuce, place the pulled pork, served with a ranch coleslaw blend and a pinch of lime juice as well as green tabasco.
9. Enjoy.

9. STIR FRY ZOODLE

Serving: 4

Preparation time: 15-22 minutes

Nutritional values: 113kcal Calories | 3g Fat | 20g Carbs | 6g Proteins

Ingredients

- Sesame oil 11/2 tsp. (or 1 tbsp. of olive oil)
- 1 bunch of thinly chopped scallions
- 2 cloves of garlic, chopped
- 1 tablespoon of fresh ginger, diced
- Two carrots, chopped into thin strands
- One red pepper bell, cut into small strands,
- Two cups of snap peas
- Four zucchini, sliced into noodles (using a utensil like this)
- 1/4 cup of soy sauce
- 3 tbsp. vinegar for rice
- 1/4 cup of fresh cilantro, diced

Directions

1. Add the oil in a wide sauté pan over medium heat. Integrate the scallions, garlic, and ginger and simmer for 1 to 2 minutes, unless aromatic.

2. Include the bell pepper, carrots, snap peas & zucchini noodles. Sauté for 5 to 6 minutes until the vegetables just start to become soft.

3. Integrate the soy sauce & rice vinegar and proceed to cook unless the vegetables are quite soft and juicy, frequently tossing, for another 3 to 4 minutes.

4. Seasoned with cilantro, serve hot.

10. TEX MEX CHICKEN SALAD

Serving: 4

Preparation time: 25 minutes

Nutritional values: 546kcal Calories | 41g Fat | 12g Carbs | 30g Proteins

Ingredients

- For the seasoning of the fajita:
- 2 tsp. of powdered chili
- 1 tsp. of cumin
- 1 tsp. of powdered garlic
- 1 teaspoon powdered onion
- 1 tsp. of paprika. smoked
- 1/2 tsp. of or to taste salt

For the fajitas

- Two spoonful's of olive oil
- 1/2 tsp. ground mustard OR 1 tbsp. of Dijon mustard as required
- 1 lemon juice
- 2 medium breasts of chicken hammered to even density
- 2 tablespoons divided butter
- 4 finely diced medium bell peppers into slices
- 1 medium red onion finely sliced into slices
- 2-3 leaves of buttered lettuce
- 2-3 leaves of romaine lettuce

To serve

- Slices of lime

- Avocado sliced

Directions

1. Mix all the ingredients for the condiments in a tiny compostable jar. Enclose well and squish. For bell peppers, save 1 1/2 tsp.

2. Integrate two tbsp. of olive oil, lemon juice, and 5 tsp. of fajita condiments in a wide, zip lock bag. In the bag, add the chicken and secure it. Push the marinade into the chicken and enable the vegetables to marinate while preparing them (or freeze in the fridge unless ready to use).

3. Cut the bell peppers as well as onions.

4. Heat 1 tbsp. of butter over moderate heat in a large skillet. Add the onions and cook for approximately 4-5 minutes, or until tender and succulent. Transfer the bell peppers and squirt 1 1/2 tsp. of fajita condiments with the restrained ones. Cook for almost 3-5 minutes if you like the peppers with a lovely crunch. And if you like it softer, end up leaving it on for about two to three minutes long. Set aside and move to a plate.

5. Melt 1 residual tablespoon of butter and brown the chicken in the same pan. Cook for 5-6 minutes, or until properly cooked.

6. In a wide salad bowl or tray, organize the lettuce and top it with chicken as well as bell peppers. Add your chosen sliced avocados, lime slices, and any other seasonings.

11. KETO BROCCOLI CHEDDAR SOUP

Serving: 4

Preparation time: 20 minutes

Nutritional values: 285kcal Calories | 25g Fat | 3g Carbs | 12g Proteins

Ingredients

- 2 spoonful's of butter

- 1/8 cup of onion, white
- 1/2 tsp. of finely chopped garlic
- 2 cups of broth of chicken
- Pepper and salt, to taste
- 1 cup of broccoli, cut into bite-sized pieces
- 1 spoon of cream cheese
- Heavy whipping cream 1/4 cup
- 1 cup of cheddar cheese, crushed
- Bacon 2 loaves, cooked and Imploded (Optional)
- 1/2 tsp. of gum xanthan (Optional)

Directions

1. Simmer the onion and garlic with butter in a wide pot over medium heat until the onions are seamless and textured.

2. Add broth as well as broccoli to the pot. Until soft, cook broccoli. Add the salt, pepper, and seasoning you want.

3. Put the cream cheese in a medium bowl and heat for ~30 seconds in the microwave until smooth and easy to mix.

4. Mix in the soup with heavy whipping cream and cream cheese; bring to the boil.

5. Turn off the heat and mix the cheddar cheese swiftly.

6. If required, stir in the xanthan gum. Allow for stiffening.

7. Serve hot with implodes of bacon (if desired)

12. SPICY THAI BUTTERNUT SQUASH SOUP

Serving: 4

Preparation time: 30 minutes

Nutritional values: 450kcal Calories | 35g Fat | 35g Carbs | 8g proteins

Ingredients

- 1 1/2 tbsp. coconut oil, refined
- 1 large onion, yellow, sliced
- 1/4 cup of a paste of red curry
- One 2-inch slice of grated or finely chopped garlic
- Four teaspoons of cloves of garlic, diced
- 4 cups vegetable stock with low sodium or water
- 1 peeled and finely diced medium butternut squash (about 4 1/2 cups)
- One 13.5-ounce coconut milk full-fat can
- 1/4 cup cashew butter or almond butter in natural form
- Lower tamari 1 tbsp.
- 1 tablespoon maple syrup or nectar of Agave
- Kosher salt about 1 tsp., plus more to flavor
- Three teaspoons of freshly pressed lemon juice
- 1/2 cup of fresh, chopped cilantro, plus more for garnishing
- Serve with coconut yogurt, roasted peanuts, scallions & sesame seeds

Directions

1. Choose the Instant Pot Sauté mode, then add the coconut oil after several minutes. When the oil is warm, add a bit of salt to the onion, and then cook for 6 to 7 minutes before it

starts to brown. Transfer the curry paste, ginger, and garlic; simmer for about 1 minute, constantly stirring, until quite tangy.

2. Spill the stock in and use a wooden spoon on the bottom of the pot to pick off some browned pieces. Stir in butternut squash, coconut milk, tamari, salt, cashew butter, and maple syrup. To blend properly, mix.

3. Shield the cover and seal the pressure release. Choose the high-pressure setting for the soup and specify the cooking time to 12 minutes.

4. Enable an organic pressure release for 5 minutes when the timer goes off, and then undergo a speedy pressure release.

5. Open the pot, add the lime juice and mix. Mix, so you have a nice and creamy broth using an electric mixer. Conversely, using a dish towel to shield the mixer cap to keep steam from spreading, you should pass the broth in batches to a mixer.

6. Stir in the minced cilantro until the broth is pureed — seasoning with coconut yogurt, peanuts, sesame seeds, and scallions as needed.

13. KETO PHO RECIPE

Serving: 4

Preparation time: 35 minutes

Nutritional values: 220kcal Calories | 5g Fat | 8g Carbs | 33g Proteins

Ingredients

- 4 Entire Star Anise
- 2 entire pods of Cardamom
- 2 entire sticks of Cinnamon
- 2 Whole Cloves
- 1 tbsp. seeds of Coriander
- 1 tsp. of ginger
- 8 cups of bone broth of beef

- 1 tablespoon of Fish sauce
- 1 tbsp. Allulose Mix of Besti Monk Fruit (optional, to taste)
- Salt (optional, to taste)

Soup Pho:

- Flank steak 12 oz. (trimmed, or sirloin)
- 2 large Zucchinis (spiraled into zoodles)

Pho toppings optional:

- Thai basil
- Cilantro
- Wedges of lime
- Slices of red chili pepper (or jalapeno peppers)
- Scallions
- Sriracha

Directions

1. For 30 minutes, put the steak in the refrigerator to make it easy to slice finely.

2. In the meantime, over moderate heat, warm a Dutch oven, minus oil. Bring the star anise, pods of cardamom, sticks of cinnamon, garlic, seeds of coriander, and fresh ginger. Toast, until aromatic, for 2-3 minutes.

3. Combine the fish sauce as well as bone broth. Mix together—Cook the pho broth and stew for 30 minutes.

4. In the meantime, to make zoodles out from the zucchini, use a spiralizer. Split the noodles from the zucchini into 4 bowls.

5. Pull it out and slice rather thinly against the grain until the steak in the refrigerator is stable. Put the steak inside each bowl on top of the zoodles.

6. Mix in the sweetener to disintegrate (if used) and modify the salt to taste whenever the broth is finished simmering. In a different pot or bowl, extract the soup. Discard all the spices that are trapped in the strainer.

7. Although the broth is already simmering, spill it over the preparing bowls instantly, making sure that the steak is immersed, so it cooks completely. (Conversely, the steak should first be stirred into the boiling broth.)

8. Thai basil, coriander, lemon slices, jalapeno or chili pepper strips, scallions, and Sriracha, and garnish with condiments of you're choosing.

14. PORK CARNITAS

Serving: 8

Preparation time: 7 hrs.15 min

Nutritional values: 442kcal Calories | 31g Fat | 9g Carbs30g Proteins

Ingredients

- 1 white, halved, and finely chopped onion
- Five cloves of garlic, chopped
- 1 jalapeño, chopped,
- 3 lbs. of cubed shoulder pork
- Salt and black pepper finely ground
- 1 tablespoon of cumin
- 2 tbsp. of fresh oregano minced
- Two Oranges
- 1 lemon
- 1/3 cup of broth of chicken

Directions

1. At the base of a slow cooker, put the onion, jalapeño garlic, pork together. Add the salt, pepper, oregano & cumin.

2. The oranges and lime are zested over the pork, then halved, and the juice is squeezed over the pork. Also, spill the broth over the pork.

3. Put the cover on and adjust the heat to medium on the slow cooker. Process for 7 hours or unless the meat is soft and quick to squash with a fork.

4. Shred the pork with two forks. The pork may be eaten instantly or frozen in an airtight jar for up to 5 days in the fridge or for up to one month in the freezer.

15. CHICKEN MEATBALLS AND CAULIFLOWER RICE WITH COCONUT HERB SAUCE

Serving: 4

Preparation time: 45 minutes

Nutritional values: 205kcal calories | 13g Fat | 3g Carbs | 20g Proteins

Ingredients

For meatballs

- Non-stick spray
- 1 tablespoon of extra virgin olive oil
- 1/2 of the red onion
- 2 cloves of garlic, chopped
- 1 lb. of ground chicken
- 1/4 cup of finely minced parsley
- 1 tablespoon of Dijon mustard
- 3/4 tsp. of kosher salt
- 1/2 tsp. of freshly ground black pepper

For sauce

- One 14-ounce of coconut milk can
- 11/4 cups of fresh, chopped parsley, distributed
- Four scallions, minced roughly
- 1 clove of garlic, peeled and crushed
- Juice and zest of one lime
- Kosher salt and black pepper, recently ground
- Red pepper flakes to serve.

- 1 Cauliflower Rice recipe

Directions

1. **Prepare the meatballs:** Set the oven to 375°F. Cover a baking sheet with aluminum foil and coat it with a non-stick spray.

2. Heat the oil in a wide skillet over medium heat. Integrate the onion and simmer until soft, about five minutes. Integrate the garlic and simmer until tangy for around 1 minute.

3. Shift the onion and garlic to a mixing saucepan and let it cool completely. Mix in chicken, parsley, and mustard, sprinkle with salt. Turn the paste into 2 tablespoon balls and shift to the parchment paper.

4. Cook the meatballs for 17 to 20 minutes until firm and fully cooked.

5. **Prepare the sauce:** In a food processor pan, blend coconut milk, scallions, parsley, garlic, lime juice & lemon zest and stir unless buttery; season with salt and pepper.

6. Cover with the red pepper flakes as well as the leftover parsley. With the sauce, end up serving over the cauliflower rice.

16. KETO RAINBOW VEGGIES AND SHEET PAN CHICKEN

Serving: 4

Preparation time: 40 minutes

Nutritional values: 380kcal Calories | 14g Fat | 35g Carbs | 31g Proteins

Ingredients

- Spray for Nonstick
- 1 lb. of boneless chicken breasts without skin
- Sesame Oil 1 tbsp.
- 2 spoonful's of soy sauce
- Honey about 2 tablespoons
- 2 bell peppers, red, chopped

- 2 bell peppers yellow, chopped

- Three carrots, diced

- 1/2 broccoli head, sliced into cloves

- 2 red, chopped onions

- Extra virgin olive oil about 2 tablespoons

- Kosher salt and black pepper, recently ground

- 1/4 cup of fresh parsley, minced, for serving

Directions

1. Heat up the oven to 400 degrees F. Slather a baking sheet lightly with non - stick spray.

2. Put the chicken on the baking tray. Stir the sesame oil and soy sauce together in a medium bowl. Dust the blend over the chicken equally.

3. On the baking dish, place the red and yellow bell peppers, broccoli, carrot & red onion. Sprinkle over the vegetables with olive oil and softly toss to coat; season with salt and pepper.

4. Roast it for 23 to 25 minutes until the veggies are soft and the chicken is thoroughly cooked. Take it out of the oven and seasoned it with parsley.

17. CAULIFLOWER POTATO SALAD

Serving: 6

Preparation time: 30-40 minutes

Nutritional values: 90kcal Calories | 4g Fat | 9g Carbs | 5g Proteins

Ingredients

- 1 head cauliflower, sliced into chunks that are bite-sized

- 3/4 cup of Greek yogurt

- 1/4 cup of sour cream

- 1 tbsp. Mustard from Dijon
- 2 tbsp. apple cider vinegar
- 1 tablespoon of fresh parsley minced
- 1 tbsp. fresh dill minced
- Celery 4 stalks, finely chopped
- 1 bunch of green, finely chopped onions
- 1/3 cup of cornichons diced
- Kosher salt and black pepper, freshly processed

Directions

1. Put the cauliflower, then coat it with water in a large container. Take the cauliflower to a simmer over moderate flame and boil until it is just fork soft, 8 to 10 minutes (do not overcook it, because, in the salad, it may not keep up).

2. Gently soak and cool the cauliflower to normal temperature. Meanwhile, mix the Greek yogurt, sour cream, mustard, vinegar, parsley, and dill together in a wide cup.

3. To incorporate, add the cauliflower, celery, green onions, and cornichons to the bowl and mix well. Sprinkle with salt & pepper.

4. When eating, chill the salad for a minimum of 1 hour. It is possible to prepare the salad 1 day in advance and keep it in the fridge until ready to eat.

18. PROSCIUTTO WRAPPED CAULIFLOWER BITES

Serving: 8-10

Preparation time: 15 minutes

Nutritional values: 215kcal Calories | 15g Fat | 5g Carbs | 15g Proteins

Ingredients

- 1 tiny cauliflower
- 1/2 cup of paste of tomatoes
- 2 spoonful's of white wine
- 1/2 tsp. of black pepper
- 1/2 cup of Parmesan cheese grated

- 20 Prosciutto slices
- 6 tbsp. of extra-virgin olive oil

Directions

1. Start preparing the cauliflower: Cut the base, and any green leaves, away from the cauliflower. Halve the cauliflower, and slice the halves into 1-inch-thick pieces. Based on the size of the slice, divide the slices into 2 or 3 bite-size bits.

2. Bring a big saucepan of salted water to a boil. In the water, parboil the cauliflower until almost soft, for 3 to 5 minutes. With paper towels, rinse the cauliflower well enough and pat off.

3. Add the tomato paste with the white wine & black pepper in a small dish to blend. On the edges of each slice of cauliflower, distribute 1 tsp., then dust with 1 tsp. of Parmesan. A prosciutto slice is carefully wrapped over each piece of cauliflower, pushing softly at the edge to seal it (it should twig well to the tomato-paste blend).

4. Continuing to work in chunks, heat two tablespoons of olive oil over moderate heat in a large pan. Add the cauliflower while the oil is hot and simmer unless the prosciutto is crispy and golden, 3 to 4 minutes on either side. Repeat till all the pieces are ready, with extra oil and cauliflower. Let it cool slowly, then serve right away.

19. CAULIFLOWER TORTILLAS

Serving: 6

Preparation time: 45 minutes

Nutritional values: 45kcal Calories | 2g Fat | 5g Carbs | 4g Proteins

Ingredients

- 1 head cauliflower
- 2 eggs, pounded lightly
- 1/2 tsp. cumin
- 1/4 tsp. of cayenne pepper

- Salt and black pepper, freshly processed, to taste

Directions

1. Heat up the oven to 375°F. Use parchment paper to cover a baking sheet.

2. Split the cauliflower into thin strips. Cut the delicate portion of the stems roughly (discard the tough and leafy parts).

3. Move the cauliflower to the mixing bowl, filling it just halfway, working in bundles. Compress the cauliflower until it looks like rice, around 45 seconds to 1 minute. Repeat for the cauliflower that remains.

4. Move the cauliflower to a dish that is microwave-safe. Microwave around 1 minute, mix well, and microwave for an extra 1 minute.

5. Move the cauliflower to a tidy kitchen towel in the center. In a twist, cover the cauliflower up. Keep the towel over the basin and curl the ends to suck the humidity out of the cauliflower.

6. Take the cauliflower back to the bowl. Add the eggs, cumin, cayenne, salt, and black pepper, and mix well.

7. Ridge the lined baking sheet with 1/4 cup of cauliflower scoops. Distribute the cauliflower into 1/8-inch-thick circles using a tiny spoon.

8. For around 8 to 9 minutes, cook the tortillas until the bottoms are crispy. Then use a spatula to turn the tortillas over cautiously and cook for another 8 to 9 minutes unless crispy on the other side.

9. The tortillas can be eaten hot, instantly, or frozen for up to five days in an airtight jar in the fridge (with parchment pieces among them).

20. KETO SALMON SUSHI BOWL

Serving: 3-4

Preparation time: 15 minutes

Nutritional values: 45kcal Calories | 6g Fat | 8g Carbs | 9g Proteins

Ingredients

- Cauliflower Rice 3/4 Cup
- Smoked salmon about 1/2 packet
- 1/2 cup of cucumber spiraled
- Avocado 1/2
- 2 sheets of seaweed-dried
- 1 teaspoon of low sodium soy sauce
- Pepper & salt, to taste
- Wasabi 1/2 teaspoon, optional

Sauce

- 3 tbsp. mayonnaise
- Sriracha 1-2 teaspoon (adjust to preference)

Direction

1. Steam the cauliflower rice and incorporate salt and black pepper (I used premade bag)
2. Put the rice layer with soy sauce as well as seasoning in the bottom of the small dish.
3. Fill the bowl with salmon, cucumber, seaweed, and avocado
4. Integrate mayo and Sriracha for sauce, adapting to the preferred heat.
5. Spread the sauce over a dish.
6. If desired, add sesame seeds as well as pepper for garnishing.

1. BAKED GARLIC PARMESAN ZUCCHINI CHIPS

Serving: 6

Preparation time: 20-30 minutes

Nutritional values: 155kcal Calories | 10g Fat | 10g Carbs | 5g Proteins

Ingredients

- Chopped 3 to 4 zucchini into pieces of 1/4-inch and 1/2-inch
- 3 tbsp. of Omega-3 DHA Extra Virgin Olive Oil STAR
- Salt to taste and freshly ground pepper
- 1 cup bread crumbs of panko
- 1/2- cup of Parmesan grated cheese
- 1 tsp. of oregano that is dried
- 1 tsp. of powdered garlic
- Cooking spray
- Non-Fat simple yogurt, for serving,

Directions

1. Preheat the cooking oven to 450.
2. Line 3 foil-based baking sheets; brush lightly with cooking spray, then set it aside.
3. Incorporate the zucchini pieces, olive oil, salt, and pepper in a wide mixing bowl; whisk until well mixed.
4. Incorporate the crumbs, cheese, oregano, plus garlic powder in a different dish.
5. Dip the zucchini pieces in the cheese mixture and cover on both ends, press to remain with the coating.
6. On the prepared baking sheets, put the slices of zucchini in a thin layer.

7. Spray every slice lightly with cooking spray. This would help to achieve a texture that is crispier.

8. Flip the pan and finish frying for 8 - 10 mints, or until the chips are nicely browned — bake for ten min.

9. Remove it from the oven.

10. With Non-Fat Simple Yogurt, serve it.

2. KETO PIZZA ROLL-UPS

Serving: 8-10

Preparation time: 15 minutes

Nutritional values: 138kcal Calories | 12g Fat | 8g Carbs | 6g Proteins

Ingredients

- 12 mozzarella cheese slices
- Chunks of pepperoni, or you may use small pepperoni as well.
- Seasoning - Italian
- Marina Sauce - Keto

Directions

1. Heat the oven to 400°F.

2. Using a baking mat and parchment paper, cover a cookie sheet.

3. Position the slices of cheese on the baking mat, then place them in the oven for 6 mints, or unless the slices of cheese tend to brown across the corners.

4. Take it out from the oven and leave to cool the cheese moderately. If you like, make the slices to chill and scatter with Italian seasoning, as well as include pepperoni.

5. With your chosen dipping sauce, wrap & serve! Enjoy

3. STUFFED MUSHROOMS WITH SAUSAGE

Serving: 8

Preparation time: 30-40 minutes

Nutritional values: 280kcal Calories | 20g Fat | 6g Carbs | 15g Proteins

Ingredients

- 1 pound of mild Italian sausage
- Cremini mushrooms about 1 pound
- 4 ounces of cream cheese
- 1/3 cup mozzarella - shredded
- Salt, as necessary
- ½ Teaspoon flakes of red pepper
- 1/4 cup of Parmesan grated cheese

Directions

1. To 350F, set the oven. Wash and cut the stems from the mushrooms.

2. Cook the sausage in a wide skillet over moderate heat. Transfer it to a wide mixing bowl until it has been cooked.

3. Add the mozzarella cheese, cream cheese, and mix to combine. Season to taste, then add salt & red pepper if required.

4. Spoon onto the mushroom caps with the sausage combination. Use Parmesan cheese for scattering. Put in a pan or casserole platter that is oven-safe.

5. Bake for 25 mints, unless the cheese is golden brown and the mushrooms are tender.

4. EASY KETO PIZZA BITES

Serving: 30

Preparation time: 30-35 minutes

Nutritional values: 82kcal Calories | 7g Fat | 1g Carbs | 4g Proteins

Ingredients

- 1 lb., cooked as well as drained Italian sausage
- Cream cheese, 4 ounces, softened.
- 1/3 of a cup of cocoa flour
- 1/2 tsp. powder for baking
- 1 tsp. of garlic diced
- 1 tsp. of seasoning - Italian
- 3 large, beaten eggs
- 1 1/4 cup mozzarella crushed

Directions

1. Preheat the oven to 350°F.
2. Mix the prepared sausage & cream cheese unless fully fused together.
3. To give the flour time to ponder the moisture, rest of the ingredients until well mixed and cool for 10 minutes.
4. If you forget to chill the dough, they will deflate while they cook and will not be pleasant round balls.
5. Use a tiny cookie scoop to transfer onto a greased baking sheet (I prefer using the silicone baking mats).
6. Bake until lightly browned for 18-20 minutes.

7. This made 30, so it depends on the scale of the scoop you're using and how closely you're packing it.

5. CUCUMBER SLICES WITH HERB AND GARLIC CHEESE

Serving: 16

Preparation time: 5 minutes

Nutritional values: 42kcal Calories | 3g Fat | 1g Carbs | 1g Proteins

Ingredients

- 1 Diced English cucumber into 16 slices
- The Chives
- 6.5 ounces of Boursin or Alouette Herb & Garlic Cheese

Directions

1. To include some novelty, cut short slices of the cucumber skin with the help of a vegetable peeler.
2. Cut the cucumber to a thickness of around 1 mm.
3. Put the cheese in a pastry bag equipped with the edge of a large star.
4. The cucumber tips could clear every moister with a paper towel pat.
5. Puff each cucumber with the cheese and cover with a piece of chives.

6. KETO POPCORN - PUFFED CHEESE

Serving: 5

Preparation: 10 minutes

Nutritional values: 80kcal Calories | 7g Fat | 0.3g Carbs | 5g Proteins

Ingredients

- cheddar 100g/3.5 ounces

Directions

1. Slice the cheese into 0.5 inches / 1 cm pieces if you use diced cheddar. If you are using a block of cheddar, crush it to the same size using your fingertips.

2. Use a cloth/kitchen towel to wrap the cheese to keep it from being gritty and let it stay for up to 3 days in a hot, dry spot. You would like the cheese to be solid and dried absolutely.

3. Preheat oven to 390 Fahrenheit / 200 Celsius. On a baking tray covered with parchment paper, spread the cheese and bake for 4-five minutes before the cheese bursts. Put a new baking tray securely over the tray to keep it from popping out over the oven.

7. BACON WRAPPED BRUSSELS SPROUTS

Serving: 4

Preparation time: 40 minutes

Nutritional values: 170kcal Calories | 15g Fat | 3g Carbs | 2g Proteins

Ingredients

12 bacon slices

12 Brussels sprouts, cut stems

Balsamic Dip:

Mayonnaise 5 tbsp.

Balsamic vinegar about 1 tbsp.

Directions

1. Preparation: Set aside baking sheets and 12 toothpicks, covered with parchment paper or a baking mat that would be non-stick — preheat the baking oven to 400 F.

2. Wrap Sprouts: Put 1 slice of bacon on each sprout of Brussels, seal it with a toothpick, and put on the baking sheet in a thin layer.

3. Bake: Bake discovered at 400 F until the bacon is translucent and the Brussels are quite juicy around 40 minutes.

4. Serve: In a medium bowl, blend the mayonnaise & balsamic vinegar altogether unless creamy. Serve Brussels sprouts covered with bacon on a plate, along with the dip.

8. KETO ASPARAGUS FRIES

Serving: 6

Preparation time: 1hour

Nutritional values: 202kcal Calories | 14g Fat | 7g Carbs | 14g Proteins

Ingredients

- 1 pound of asparagus chopped (thick if possible)
- Salt and pepper to taste

- 1 cup of Parmesan cheese
- 3/4 cup of almond flour
- 1/4 tsp. of cayenne pepper
- 1/4 tsp. of baking powder
- 4 pounded eggs
- avocado oil spray

Directions

1. Use a fork to cut the asparagus spikes with gaps—season well with a minimum of 1/2 teaspoon of salt. Put on paper towels and let it rest for 30 minutes.

2. In the meantime, mix 1 cup of Parmesan, cayenne pepper, almond flour & baking powder in a dish. Sprinkle with salt to taste.

3. Pound the egg in a different dish.

4. Soak the asparagus segments in the eggs, then cover with the blend of the cheese.

5. Your air fryer should be preheated to 400 degrees.

6. Organize the asparagus in one layer and, if required, cook in chunks. Spray the oil well— Cook for five minutes. Turn, and then respray.

7. Fry unless the asparagus is soft for the next 4 or 5 minutes.

9. EGG, BACON, AND CHEESE SLIDERS

Serving: 6

Preparation time: 10 minutes

Nutritional values: 237kcal Calories | 18g Fat | 3g Carbs | 15g Proteins

Ingredients

- 6 peeled, boiled eggs

- 6 Thin cheddar cheese strips
- 3 Slices of bacon that has been cooked
- 1/2 of Avocado
- 1/2 teaspoon Juice of a lime
- 1/2 Teaspoon cumin

Directions

1. In a mixing bowl, place 1/2 of an avocado.
2. Stir in the cumin as well as lime juice. Mix until completely smooth. To taste, incorporate the salt.
3. Cut each hardboiled egg lengthwise in half.
4. Put on the lower half of the egg one piece of thinly cut cheddar cheese.
5. Place 1/2 a slice of cooked bacon on edge.
6. On the edge of the bacon, put a spoonful of the avocado mixture on top.
7. To make a little sandwich, place the remaining half of the egg face right over the top. Protect the bite of the egg with a toothpick placed down the center.
8. For your remaining eggs, replicate steps 4-7.
9. Add salt and pepper to each bite of the egg to taste & serve.

10. TURKEY BACON WRAP RANCH PINWHEELS

Serving: 6

Preparation time: 15 minutes

Nutritional values: 133kcal Calories | 12g Fat | 2g Carbs | 5g proteins

Ingredients

- 6 ounces of cheese cream
- 12 strips of smoked turkey deli (about 3 oz.)

- 1/4 teaspoon powdered garlic
- 1/4 teaspoon of chopped dried onion
- Dried dill weed 1/4 teaspoon
- 1 tablespoon of crumbling bacon
- 2 tablespoons cheddar shredded cheese

Directions

1. Among 2 pieces of plastic wrap, place the cream cheese. Stretch it out until it's approximately 1/4 inch thick. Scrape the plastic wrap off the top piece. On top of the cream cheese, place the slices of turkey on the edge.

2. Cover and switch the whole item over with a fresh layer of plastic wrap. Chop off the plastic bit that is on the upper right now. Slather it on top of the cream cheese with the seasoning. Spray it with cheese and bacon.

3. Roll the pinwheels up such that the exterior is the turkey. Refrigerate for 2 minimum hours. On the edge of low-carb crackers or diced cucumber, cut into 12 bits and serve.

2.4 Keto Desserts

1. KETO BROWN BUTTER PRALINES

Serving: 10

Preparation time: 16 minutes

Nutritional values: 338kcal Calories | 36g Fat | 3g Carbs | 2g Proteins

Ingredients

- 2 Salted butter sticks
- Heavy cream 2/3 cup
- 2/3 Cup of Sweetener Granular 1/2 tsp. of xanthan gum
- 2 Cups Pecans diced

- Maldon Sea salt

Directions

1. Use parchment paper or a silicone baking mat to make a cookie sheet.

2. Cook the butter in a skillet over medium flame, stirring regularly. It's going to take less than five min. Whisk in the heavy cream, sweetener, and xanthan gum. Extract it from the heat.

3. Mix in the nuts and put in the fridge, stirring regularly, for 1 hour to tighten up. The mixture's going to get really dense. Scrape onto the prepared baking sheet into 10 cookie styles and spray, if necessary, with the Maldon salt. Let the baking sheet freeze until frozen.

4. Store and keep stored in the fridge until served in an airtight dish.

2. KETO CHOCOLATE MOUSSE

Serving: 4

Preparation time: 10 minutes

Nutritional values: 220kcal Calories | 25g Fat | 5g Carbs | 2g Proteins

Ingredients

- 1 Cup of Whipped Heavy Cream
- 1/4 cup Cocoa powder unsweetened, sifted
- 1/4 Cup Sweetener Powdered
- 1 tsp. extract of vanilla
- Kosher salt about 1/4 teaspoon

Directions

1. Use the cream to whip into stiff peaks. Include the cocoa powder, vanilla, sweetener, and salt, then mix until all the products are mixed.

3. KETO CHEESECAKE FLUFF

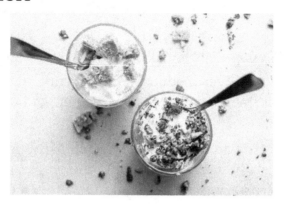

Serving: 6

Preparation time: 10 minutes

Nutritional values: 260kcal Calories | 27g Fat | 4g Carbs | 4g Proteins

Ingredients

- 1 Cup of Whipping Heavy Cream
- 1 Eight oz. Cream Cheese Brick, Softened
- 1 Lemon Zest
- 1/2 Cup of Sweetener Granular

Directions

1. In a stand mixer, combine the heavy cream as well as stir until stiff peaks are made. A hand blender or a whisk can also be used by hand using a whisk.

2. In a different bowl, scrape the whipped cream and put it aside.

3. In the stand blender bowl, add the textured cream cheese, zest, and sweetener, then beat until sturdy.

4. With the cream cheese, add the whipped cream into the stand blender dish. Mix carefully until it is halfway mixed with a spatula. To finish whipping until sturdy, use the stand mixer.

5. Serve with a favorite topping of you.

4. LOW CARB BLUEBERRY CRISP

Serving: 2

Preparation time: 20-25 minutes

Nutritional values: 390kcal Calories | 35g Fat | 17g Carbs | 6g Proteins

Ingredients

- 1 Cup of Fresh or Frozen Blueberries
- 1/4 Cup Halves of Pecan
- Almond Meal/Flour 1/8 cup
- Butter around 2 tbsp.
- Granular Sweetener 2 tablespoons - distributed
- 1 tablespoon of flax
- Cinnamon 1/2 Teaspoon
- ½ teaspoon Extract from vanilla
- Kosher salt about 1/4 teaspoon
- Heavy cream 2 tablespoons

Directions

1. Heat the oven to 400F.
2. Put 1/2 cup of blueberries and 1/2 tablespoons of swerve sweetener in 2, 1 cup ramekins. Blend and combine.
3. Incorporate the pecans, almond flour, butter, 1 tbsp. sweetener, cinnamon, ground flax, vanilla, and kosher salt into the food processor. Pulse while you mix the ingredients.
4. Place on top of the blueberries with the blend. Put the ramekins on a baking sheet and cook for 15-20 minutes in the middle of the oven or until the topping turn's toasty brown. Serve with 1 tablespoon of heavy cream slathered on top of each one.

5. 1 MINT LOW CARB BROWNIE

Serving: 1

Preparation time: 3 minutes

Nutritional values: 196kcal Calories | 17g Fat | 2g Carbs | 8g Proteins

Ingredients

- 2 tablespoons almond flour
- 1 tablespoon of preferred granulated sweetener
- 1 tablespoon powdered cocoa
- Baking Powder 1/8 teaspoon
- Almond butter 1 tablespoon. * See notes
- 3 tablespoons of milk, unsweetened almond milk,
- 1 tablespoon of chocolate chips of preference - optional

Directions

1. A tiny microwave-protected cereal bowl or ramkin is lightly greased with cooking spray and placed aside.

2. Integrate all of your dried ingredients in a medium mixing bowl and blend well.

3. Integrate the creamy almond butter and milk in a separate bowl and mix them together. Place the wet and dry ingredients together and blend properly. Roll them through if chocolate chips are used.

4. Microwave at intervals of 30 seconds until the optimal texture has been reached. Take from the microwave then, before eating, let settle for one min.

6. KETO PEANUT BUTTER BALLS

Joy Filled Eats

Serving: 18

Preparation time: 20 minutes

Nutritional values: 195kcal Calories | 17g Fat | 7g Carbs | 7g Proteins

Ingredients

- 1 cup of finely diced salted peanuts (not peanut flour)
- 1 cup of peanut butter
- 1 cup of sweetener powdered, like swerve
- 8-ounce chocolate chips free from sugar

Directions

1. Combine the diced peanuts, peanut butter, and the sweetener, respectively. Distribute the 18-piece crust and mold it into balls. Put them on a baking sheet covered with wax paper. Put it in the fridge until they're cold.

2. In the oven or on top of a dual boiler, heat the chocolate chips. Mix chocolate chips in the microwave, swirling every 30 seconds till they are 75percent melted. Then stir before the remainder of it melts.

3. Soak the chocolate for each peanut butter ball and put it back on the wax paper. Until the chocolate settles, put it in the fridge.

7. WHITE CHOCOLATE PEANUT BUTTER BLONDIES

Serving: 16

Preparation time: 35 minutes

Nutritional values: 105kcal Calories | 9g Fat | 2g Carbs | 3g Proteins

Ingredients

- 1/2 cup of peanut butter
- Softened butter around 4 tablespoons
- Two Eggs
- Vanilla 1 teaspoon
- 3 tbsp. fresh cocoa butter melted
- 1/4 cup of almond flour
- 1 tablespoon of coconut flour
- 1/2 cup sweetener
- 1/4 cup of fresh cocoa butter diced

Directions

1. Preheat the baking oven to 350. Use cooking spray to cover the base of a 9 into 9 baking tray.

2. Beat the first 5 ingredients with an electric mixer until creamy. Bring the flour, sweetener, and sliced cocoa butter into the mixture. Scattered in a baking dish that has been prepared. Bake until the middle no longer jostles, and the corners are golden, for 25 minutes.

3. Cool thoroughly, and then, before slicing, chill in the freezer for 2-3 hours.

8. LOW CARB BAKED APPLES

Serving: 4

Preparation time: 20 minutes

Nutritional values: 340kcal Calories | 88g Fat | 8g Carbs | 4g Proteins

Ingredients

- 2 ounces. cheese,
- 1 oz. Walnuts or Pecans
- 4 tablespoon coconut flour
- Cinnamon 1⁄2 tsp.
- Vanilla extract around 1⁄4 teaspoon
- One tart/sour apple

To serve

- 3⁄4 cup of heavy whipped cream
- Vanilla extract about 1⁄2 teaspoon

Directions

1. Heat the oven to 175°C (350°F). In a crispy dough, mix the hot butter, diced almonds, coconut flour, cinnamon & vanilla together.
2. Wash the apple, but don't eliminate the seeds or chop it. Cut both edges off and cut 4 slices through the center portion.
3. In a greased baking dish, put the slices and place dough crumbs on top. Bake fifteen minutes or more or until light brown appears on the crumbs.
4. To a moderate bowl, incorporate heavy whipping cream as well as vanilla and whisk until soft peaks appear.
5. For a minute or two, let the apples chilled and serve with a spoonful of whipped cream.

9. FROZEN YOGURT POPSICLES

Serving: 12

Preparation time: 10mins 2hours

Nutritional values: 73kcal Calories | 60g Fat | 28g Carbs | 13g Proteins

Ingredients

- 8 oz. Mango chilled, chopped
- 8 oz. Strawberries chilled
- 1 cup of Greek full-fat yogurt
- 1/2 cup of heavy whipped cream
- 1 teaspoon extract of vanilla

Directions

1. Let the strawberries and mango defrost for 10 to 15 minutes.
2. In a mixer, place all the materials and combine until creamy.
3. End up serving as fluffy ice cream instantly or pipe into Popsicle shapes and chill for at least a few hours. If you do have an ice cream machine, it can be used, of course.

10. CHOCOLATE AVOCADO TRUFFLES

Serving: 20

Preparation time: 35 minutes

Nutritional values: 65kcal Calories | 76g Fat | 19g Carbs | 5g Proteins

Ingredients

- 1 (7 ounces.) ripe, diced avocado
- Vanilla extract about 1/2 teaspoon
- 1/2 lemon, zest
- About 1 pinch of salt
- Five ounces. Dark chocolate containing cocoa solids of at least 80 percent, finely diced
- 1 spoonful of coconut oil
- 1 tbsp. cocoa powder unsweetened

Directions

1. Use an electric mixer to mix the avocado and vanilla extract. The use of ripe avocado is necessary in order for the mixture to be fully creamy.
2. Add a tablespoon of salt and mix in the lemon zest.
3. In boiling water or oven, melt the chocolate & coconut oil.
4. Incorporate the chocolate & avocado and blend properly. Let it rest for 30 minutes in the fridge or until the batter is compact but not fully solid.
5. With your fingertips, shape little truffle balls. Likewise, use two teaspoons or a tiny scoop. Morph and roll in the cocoa powder with the hands.

11. CRUNCHY KETO BERRY MOUSSE

Serving: 8

Preparation time: 10 minutes

Nutritional values: 256kcal Calories | 26g Fat | 3g Carbs | 2g Proteins

Ingredients

- Two cups of heavy whipped cream
- Three ounces. Fresh strawberries or blueberries or raspberries
- 2 oz. Pecans diced
- 1/2 of a lime, zest
- Vanilla extract around 1/4 teaspoon

Directions

1. Drop the cream into a container and whip until soft peaks appear using a hand mixer. Towards the top, add the lime zest, then vanilla.

2. Cover the whipped cream with berries & nuts and stir thoroughly.

3. Wrap with plastic and allow for 3 or even more hours for a stable mousse to settle in the fridge. While you don't like a less firm consistency, you can also experience the dessert instantly.

Conclusion

Ketogenic' is a name for a diet that is low-carb. The concept is for you to obtain more protein and fat calories and fewer carbs. You reduce much of the carbs, such as sugar, coffee, baked goods, and white bread that are easily digestible.

If you consume fewer than 50 g of carbs a day, the body can gradually run out of resources (blood sugar) that you can use instantly. Usually, this takes 3 or 4 days. Then you're going to start breaking down fat and protein for nutrition, which will help with weight loss. This is classified as ketosis.

A ketogenic diet plan intended to induce ketosis, disintegrate body fat into ketones and enable the body to perform on ketones instead of glucose to a great extent. Since samen is the ultimate aim of these diets, there are typically a lot of connections between the various forms of the ketogenic diet, especially in terms of being low in carbohydrates and high in dietary fat. A program that focuses on high-fat and low carbohydrates is the Ketogenic Diet, and it has many advantages.

It is necessary to remember that a short-term diet that emphasizes weight reduction rather than medical benefits is a ketogenic diet. To reduce weight, people use a keto diet more commonly, although it may help treat some medical problems, such as epilepsy, too. People with heart problems, some neurological disorders, and also acne can even be supported, although further research in those fields needs to be conducted.

CPSIA information can be obtained
at www.ICGtesting.com
Printed in the USA
LVHW050256300321
682893LV00019B/1137